Taos Institute Publications

The Taos Institute is a nonprofit organization dedicated to the development of social constructionist theory and practice for purposes of world benefit. Constructionist theory and practice locate the source of meaning, value, and action in communicative relations among people. Our major investment is in fostering relational processes that can enhance the welfare of people and the world in which they live. Taos Institute Publications offers contributions to cutting-edge theory and practice in social construction. Our books are designed for scholars, practitioners, students, and the openly curious public. The **Focus Book Series** provides brief introductions and overviews that illuminate theories, concepts, and useful practices. The **Tempo Book Series** is especially dedicated to the general public and to practitioners. The **Books for Professionals Series** provides in-depth works that focus on recent developments in theory and practice. **WorldShare Books** is an online offering of books in PDF format for free download from our website. Our books are particularly relevant to social scientists and to practitioners concerned with individual, family, organizational, community, and societal change.

— Kenneth J. Gergen
President, Board of Directors
The Taos Institute

For information about the Taos Institute and social constructionism visit:
www.taosinstitute.net

70Candles!

Women Thriving in Their 8th Decade

By
Jane Giddan and Ellen Cole

Taos Institute Publications
Chagrin Falls, Ohio
USA

70Candles! Women Thriving in Their 8th Decade

Library of Congress Catalog Card Number: 2015945118

Designed by: Debbi Stocco

Taos Institute Publications
A Division of the Taos Institute
Chagrin Falls, Ohio
USA

ISBN-10: 1-938552-35-0
ISBN-13: 978-1-938552-35-9 (paperback)   Printed in the USA and in the UK

TABLE OF CONTENTS

Foreword 6

Introduction 8

Chapter One: The Blogs Speak 18

Chapter Two: 70Candles Gatherings 58

Chapter Three: Pulling It All Together 103

Chapter Four: What Do the Experts Say? 118

Chapter Five: What Lies Ahead? 132

Appendices 156

References 165

Acknowledgments 176

Additional Reading 177

Relevant Websites 180

About the Authors 181

FOREWORD

The demographic deluge across the western world, known as the "Baby Boomer wave," is now flooding the over-60 terrain. Many of the "Babies" are now celebrating their 70th birthday, as of 2015. Their reputation, which has followed them throughout their lives, is that they are societal game changers. The power of their numbers has made an impact on all facets of cultural life. For now, this generation is engaged in a monumental act—the reconstruction of what it means to be "old." The traditional definition that aging means loss, degeneration, and irrelevancy is not acceptable to them. They have always enjoyed the spotlight, as a powerful and large cohort, and they are not content to lose it now. They are eager to change what it means to be "old." They are engaged in a social reconstruction of enormous magnitude; it is a daring endeavor with great promise for the future.

The present work is a precious gift to all of us who are someday hoping to become 70, or who are already there. Its central themes are harbingers of new and dramatically different definitions of what it means to age. The contributors to this work offer invitations to the Baby Boomers, who are a half-step behind them in years. The volume is being published as part of the Taos Institute's WorldShare Books for several important reasons. First, it is an illustration of construction-ism in action, as people join together to create a new and promising way of looking at the world. By dropping in on these invigorating conversations, we as readers can discover the many ways in which aging—despite the normal struggles inherent in any developmental change—can be a period of growth and wonderment. A new construc-tion of aging, one that is more positive than anything that has come before it, is a wonderful thing. How this vision becomes alive and then transformative is worthy of a reader's attention. We see in detail how it may be accomplished.

WorldShare Books was created to provide electronic resources freely to the people of the world. *70Candles! Women Thriving in Their 8th Decade* is an example of the Taos Institute's mission as a non-profit educational organization, dedicated to promoting a social constructionist approach to personal and professional life. This is an uplifting book to read, as it encourages each of us to explore and discover what positive aging may mean to us. I recommend the book, heartily.

Mary Gergen
Editor, WorldShare Books

INTRODUCTION

The mission of positive aging is very clear:
to add more life to years, not just more years to life.

George V. Vaillant, 2004

The idea for this book began to germinate when we, Jane and Ellen, were about to turn seventy. A miracle, we thought. How on this good earth had we gone from being best pals at age 14 to our new term of endearment—old ladies! Needless to say, we were curious about what lay ahead. What does it look like and feel like, we wondered, to be a 70 year old woman today? Are our peers still working for paychecks? If not, how do they identify themselves, particularly those, like us, with meaningful careers? And above all, what brings satisfaction and joy in one's 70's? How are women thriving and flourishing as they enter and proceed through their eighth decade? And so began, with questions and curiosity, our 70Candles project.

It occurred to us that it might be really fun and instructive to gather together 70 year-old women for face-to-face exchanges. We thought of the focus group model, the small group technique typically used by marketers to evaluate customer response to a new product, or by social scientists who want to understand why people hold certain beliefs. We quickly decided to call our gatherings "conversation groups," hoping to set an informal, very supportive and friendly tone.

To-date we have conducted eight such groups: in Philadelphia, Dallas (2), New York City (2), Albany, NY, (2), and Ithaca, NY.

After just the first gathering (in Philadelphia), we realized we had stumbled onto something much more meaningful than we had anticipated. Reminded of the consciousness-raising groups that some of us had experienced in our 20's and 30's, we realized that gathering together these same women, now at least four decades later, had a similar effect. Yes, we collected information, but it turned out to be the participants (and we count ourselves among them) who were the real benefactors.

OUR TURNING SEVENTY

Our friendship began when we were 14 and was always filled with adventures. Through the decades that followed, we stayed in touch. Marriages, babies, moves to different cities…nothing disrupted our connection; and like dear old friends everywhere, as soon as we were together again, we just picked up where we left off.

In more recent years, when I, Jane, visited Ellen in Anchorage Alaska, the first thing she asked was, "Are you ready for an adventure?" Off we flew to the Kenai Peninsula, boated across pristine Kachemak Bay, and joined her friends in a wooded cabin overlooking Halibut Cove. It was a picture perfect scene. It was gorgeous and thrilling.

Between us, we have crisscrossed the country, Jane living in New York, California, Florida, Ohio, and now Dallas; Ellen in New York, Boston, New Mexico, Arizona, Anchorage, and now Albany. These most recent moves will frame our elder years. After retiring from university careers, Jane and her husband resettled to Dallas to be near the families of their two children and three grandchildren. Ellen and her husband moved for his "post-retirement job" as Head-of-School at the independent day-school he attended as a child, fortuitously near three of their four children and other family members. We've both faced the challenges of leaving old pals behind and creating new friendships, and re-designing our work lives. We're both, happily, more involved with our grandchildren than ever before.

Here were our thoughts and feelings as we reached our 70th birthdays:

Jane

But this one is bigger than the rest. Turning 70 feels awesome, somehow daunting, and unbelievable. My mother said at 60, "You feel like the same person you always were." She was right, I do. I don't feel old or elderly. Remember how old 70 year-olds used to seem?

We women who entered the work force in new, large numbers during the second wave of feminism are now facing choices about our work lives. Okay, I admit it. I'm afraid to stop working. I can't imagine life on the "other side" of my work life. My career, as a speech-language pathologist and professor, has lasted 50 years so far, and has fascinated me and served me well. I enjoyed all aspects of my previous teaching, writing, clinical role in a Department of Psychiatry. I still love to teach children to talk. I'm in flow during those intriguing therapy sessions, where I feel I'm serving an important purpose and my skills are valued. Appointments shape my days and focus.

Recently, however, there was an alteration in a growing home health company I work for in my new city. As the business expanded, more layers of authority were inserted to keep track of paper work and morale. Suddenly I was being supervised by a sweet, energetic millennial, young enough to be my granddaughter. I had been with the company, mentoring others, and requiring little oversight, in my post-post-career evolution, longer than she had been out of graduate school. To my chagrin, I started receiving joyful notes written in pink and green ink, with smiley faces, little hearts and multiple exclamation marks cheering my fine record keeping. Was this generational mismatch the sign I'd been waiting for? I decided it was, and shifted gears, to an on-call mentoring role. Semi-retirement…edging toward the real deal.

Eager to meet people closer to my age in this city still new to me, and to find new activities in my semi-retirement era, I searched the local newspaper for clues to previously unexplored terrain. When I saw listings for the local Senior Center I paused, but I didn't feel "ready" to acknowledge that my 70 plus years would certainly qualify me as a member.

My worst fears fell by the wayside. I actually experienced a painless and rather pleasant entry into what quickly reminded me of summer camp. Men and women, roughly of my age group, and many in their fifties, entertained themselves at an array of activities in a comfortable, well-equipped center. Food, sports, arts, crafts, music, languages, cards, and mah-jongg, you name it. Want to travel? Just sign up. Want to take responsibility for running the place? Volunteer. Offer charitable assistance in the community, along with others? No problem. Sing? Dance? Exercise? Socialize? Just check the monthly calendar. What was I afraid of?

I gave myself permission to be a dabbler in my eighth decade. My mother always told me that the various pursuits of my youth would forever be a part of me. She predicted that all those lessons would pay off some day. As an adult, I would certainly have a full menu of things I could do…piano? guitar? dance? sports? Maybe the time had come to cash in those valuable childhood chips.

Energized, I next set off to try my hand at oil painting. I'd tried acrylic paint years ago…My autumn forest picture, painted in the Sierras in our early married days, stayed among my treasured possessions until our next to last move…I loved its orange tall-tree grandeur. I put on my old black work scrubs, gathered my required roll of paper towels, and off I went, to a newer Senior Center, in another town, where large sun-lit rooms were busy with a variety of activities. Our group of ten sat quietly at two rows of tables facing the instructor's easel. He had prepared a small canvas set upon a table easel, one for each of us, with a vinyl palette chromatically arranged with all the paints needed for the day's project. The class was quiet while the white-haired instructor told us exactly what we needed to do, each step of the way, as we created an "Italian Villa." He was most patient and clear as he guided our progress. Lessons about perspective, the use of the brushes, and hints on mixing and applying paint were sprinkled throughout the morning.

Most important for health of course is staying fit, so I joined an exercise class led by a talented trainer. As I looked in the mirror during my 8:30 A.M. exercise class I saw a room of brightly clad 50ish year old women, intense in their efforts to stay trim and fit. There in the front row, up close to better hear and see, I viewed myself, in all-purpose black, standing tall, balancing well on one foot while I palmed green seven pound barbells. Clearly the oldest person as far as the eye could see, but I felt rather...ageless.

As I put away my weights and mat one morning, Lindy approached to tell me yet again that I was her "hero." This time, however, she explained why. She confided that her mother was old and weak and sad at 73, and that was what she imagined her old age would be like. She said, as she watched me, I inspired her to think differently about getting old. Her words moved me to my core.

I began to notice an interesting reversal after my husband's retirement and during the reduction in my formal work life and separation from my long career. What used to be background, jumped to the foreground of our daily existence. Time, that valuable commodity, previously carved and assigned in calendared bits, was wondrously unleashed.

Breakfast and wake-up routines definitely changed. In place of quick showers, dressing, a bite of food, and then out the door, my husband and I now enjoyed an extended A.M. coffee, a real breakfast, and attentively read the entire newspaper.

We had an agreement—I cooked the first 25 years, and he was to cook the second 25, so I was sous-chef for now. But my turn was coming up again!

Doctors' visits? They used to be occasional events. I welcomed the reminder calls for appointments made months in advance. Now, much to my dismay, doctors and dentists seemed to alert us with greater frequency for some kind of check-up or other. Who knew you could need so much medical attention—a specialist for every body part! And, oh yes, bring a sweater, because those waiting rooms are cold.

I've become the techie for my husband's Cult Classics Publisher literary web sites and related social media, a steep learning curve for me; and oh yes, the 70Candles blog and project have kept me happily immersed for long stretches of time.

We moved to this new city to be near our two children and three grandchildren. It has been a treat to be part of their lives and to watch the children grow. We're glad too that they have gotten to know us better as we've built archival memories together.

Ellen

I turned 70 two and a half months ago. It's taken me this long to sit down and write about it. Yes, I always procrastinate; it's the way I handle stressful situations. But this time I also believe I needed the distance. Turning 70 represented a profound shift for me, much like my memory of turning 30. When I turned 30 I realized I was a grown-up. I guess that meant, okay you're responsible (as in weighty responsibility) now. I told everyone I knew to ignore my birthday, and when they did I was devastated. Seventy felt equally onerous as it approached, but this time I admitted that I wanted a big fuss. My family came through for me in spades, for which I am deeply grateful. But still…70…from grown-up to old lady in 24 hours. I thought it would be a big deal. It was. It is.

I can't wear high heels anymore. Many women wouldn't care about this, but I attend a lot of dress-up events, and host many of them at my home, and NO ONE makes dressy flats that are comfortable, at least for my feet. I hike and walk long distances (like marathons), and maybe the hardest old lady problem of all is having to—as one woman put it just this morning—wiz every other second, it seems. I know there are pills for "incontinence," but I'm not that bad yet, and am medicine-avoidant, to boot. So I've become shameless about peeing in the woods and around the corner from everywhere.

The biggest issue for me was work. By chance, my husband's acceptance of a new job in a new state coincided with my turning 70. Most 70-year-old professionals have the opportunity and the time to contemplate retirement, if it's not already a fait accompli, but I didn't have that opportunity. I stayed in Alaska and kept working for six months after my husband moved to New York for his new position, but in no way did either of us want a long distance (extra-long in our case) relationship, and we were both thrilled about this new opportunity for him. So I left a position I loved. I wasn't ready to leave, and I certainly wasn't ready to stop working full-time, although it was the right move to make. I decided at age 70, already having earned a PhD decades ago, to go back to graduate school for a year and get a second master's degree in a new branch of my field—a GREAT decision for me. But it was and is very, very, weird not to have an office, a responsible position, a title, and most of all a salary. It is very, very, weird when I'm asked by some receptionist or other, either the name of my employer or "Are you retired?" These questions make me want to scream. Or sob. And I know, when I'm gentle with myself, that my angst is related to the fact that I didn't have the chance to retire on my own time table, at least not yet.

Being a grandma is as rewarding as everyone says it is, and more. When my granddaughter called me a few months ago and invited me to sleep in her "spare bed" I almost cried with happiness (I couldn't do that if I was still in Alaska). When our grandson suggested last night that we see *Pirates of the Caribbean,* of course my husband and I went even though it would have been last on our list. When another granddaughter wound up getting a mysterious illness after returning from Ghana, we could actually go to the hospital and cheer her up. When our two little grandsons gave us a wind chime to hang outside our kitchen door, our taste or not, you bet we hung it up where we see it every morning, afternoon, and evening. It is fun being geographically closer to grandchildren, even without a familiar career-identity.

At 70 I was the oldest-by-far student in the University of Pennsylvania's Masters in Positive Psychology program. Since graduating, I have used my new and old skills to teach high school students (for the first time), college students, and doctoral students. In two months I will begin a new full-time position as a professor at a local college, working primarily with graduate students in Mental Health Counseling. It is much like the position I left in Alaska—my dream job.

Indeed, 70 affords us the opportunity to recreate our lives—that is a beautiful truth. For me it has included a geographical move and leaving a position before I was ready to do so. My re-creation at this moment, and for the near future, is returning to full-time work that I have done for decades, work that I love. I want to continue to contribute to the world in ways that I can, and I want to use my brain and my creativity. I laugh a lot in the classroom. I love professional colleagues. I am lucky enough that I was offered a position at my age—I'm still pinching myself.

MOVING FORWARD

Although we have taken somewhat different paths, we both agree that turning 70 and entering our eighth decade has, indeed, been momentous. Do you remember what it was like to enter adolescence—that double digits was a significant marker? Similarly, 30 said, "Welcome to adulthood," 50 "Welcome to mid-life." And now 70, "Welcome to old age." We have found this new era both exciting and scary. Developmental psychologists speak of life's stages and phases and rites of passage, and perhaps the purpose of this book is the recognition that 70 is something, something important, part of a new stage of life, not just a birthday like any other.

THE PLAN

As you will see, the book is organized as follows: In Chapter One, women spoke to us, and to each other, through the 70Candles. com blog. We compile and illustrate themes from the blog and present excerpts and selected entries. It is anecdotal evidence.

Chapter Two introduces you to the 70Candles gatherings—conversation groups we held across the country, to listen to our peers discuss this era in their lives. We tell how we organized these 2-hour conversation groups, how they were conducted, and what they looked and felt like.

Chapter Three explores the various themes discussed in those 70Candles face-to-face gatherings. We summarize the lessons learned, note business mentioned as still unfinished, and create a composite picture of the 70Candles woman as we envision a new Senior Adult Stage of development.

In Chapter Four we look to the past as we briefly review some pertinent literature. These readings, historic and current, scientific and popular, served as a backdrop for this project.

Chapter Five is our view toward the future, both for individuals and for society, as we are all impacted by the new longevity explosion. We examine current research, technology, and social policy to get an idea about what the decades ahead might be like.

A mea culpa is in order here. It was only after several readers mentioned it that we realized an omission in the pages that follow. We neither asked about nor did women volunteer to talk about sex in the eighth decade. The research is clear that, in the words of Karl Pillemer, "the spark changes," but it is not extinguished. And it is clear to us that this is a topic we want to explore much, much more. Stay tuned!

We hope you find inspiration for growth ahead in this new, eighth decade for women, and we hope that you come away from reading our book with the sense that you have been part of this conversation. We pull the pieces together expecting that you will have not a road map, but a practical and positive guide at your side as you traverse your seventies. Your guide is actually a compilation of the hundreds of women who have shared their lives with us over the past few years—as professional writers, bloggers, and conversation group attendees. We are extremely grateful to them and to you, our readers.

CHAPTER ONE

The Blogs Speak

*There's a sense that time is precious and you should
enjoy and thrive in what you're doing to the hilt.*

Ruth Bader Ginsburg

So there we were, near 70, both facing major moves with our
spouses, significant career alterations, and new family involve-
ments. We felt the need for some kind of road map for these
transitional years and for the era ahead. We were aware that the average life-span for women in America was now 81, and many of us could
expect to live to 100, but it was hard to imagine this extended longevity for ourselves. What were women in their eighth decade doing with
their time? What were their hopes, dreams, and expectations? What
does "old" look like these days? After culling the literature and reading what researchers had to say, we decided to find more personal
answers another way. We would ask women themselves through an
online blog we decided to call 70Candles (70Candles.com).

In this chapter we begin with the blog's welcome greeting and
then share selected entries that seem to best represent the spirit of the
submissions we received. You will see that many of the entries can
be categorized into common themes, which are reflected upon again
in the discussion groups. We end the chapter with a more creative
approach to the eighth decade from a few readers. First, here is our
opening statement that appears on the blog's homepage:

Women everywhere, welcome to our blogspot, a space for sharing experiences, thoughts, and ideas about how to overcome obstacles and thrive as we approach and endure in the eighth decade of life. We hope this exchange will be a source of inspiration for the next generation of seventy year olds. Those baby boomers are hot on our heels, and want to know more about what lies ahead. Nobody gave us a guidebook or shared what this path might be like. As we burn those seventy candles, we can help shed some light on the trail for them.

What has this transition been like for you? Serious, funny, commonplace, unusual, short, long stories, all are welcome. How does it feel to be among the oldest in the crowd? What does it take to thrive in this decade? How do you think others see you? What contributes to well-being and yes, flourishing at three score and ten?

We welcome the comments and reflections of women everywhere. All cultures, ethnicities, socioeconomic status and backgrounds; as diverse a sample as we can reach.

Please contribute brief anecdotes, observations, thoughts, ideas, and life stories by posting them in the comment section below.

Alternatively, you could email longer stories to us at: 70Candles@gmail.com. Please include information about your age, ethnicity/cultural background, geographic location, education, and work status. We will organize, collate, and share your emailed stories anonymously on this blogspot. Ultimately this may become a book about how our generation flourishes. Spread the word!!

Soon, women began to respond. Postings arrived from various parts of the U.S., but also from as far away as Australia, New Zealand, London, and Tel Aviv. Women wrote, often at length, about a variety of personal thoughts and concerns.

The comments and posts arrived, slowly at first, then gathered momentum as women began to talk and lend support to each other on our site. We have disguised their names in the entries below, to preserve anonymity. Women reaching their 70th birthday, idly searching the web for comfort, found us and shared thoughts about that threshold in their lives. Others, near or in their seventies, or just thinking about getting older, shared personal anecdotes, told tales about ageism, and described retirement struggles, financial calamities, and crises over moving. Many more offered encouragement and spoke of new projects, gratitude, and resilience. As you will see, the entries were rich with honest emotions, sensitive observations, and yes, good humor.

Most apparent, was the emotional urge to connect. Our bloggers expressed the pleasure they felt at being able to share with other women who might resonate with similar feelings and concerns. And these, by the way, were the same sentiments we later heard expressed in our discussion groups. You can sense the relief in some of the entries:

Reaching Out

Thank God, I am not alone!

I knew there were active, intelligent, aging, seeking women out there who haven't given up in this quest for happiness and the fulfilled life!

I have bookmarked this site and plan on becoming a regular visitor…I have found someone to talk to.

I love how you are facing 70. Thanks for sharing. I am also 69 and just seeing somebody else with that number was for some strange reason reassuring…

Thank you for this opportunity for me and any women seventy-ish to share their stories…

…The way I found your site is by googling, out of desperation, how does a seventy year old make a decision to move, or something like that. Anyway, I kinda think it was fate that brought me to your site and I think it's wonderful that you've started it.

There have been remarkably eloquent entries about the prospect of turning 70. As that landmark birthdate approached, women somehow learned about our site from others, or idly Googled "70," and up would pop the link to our blog. It seemed a safe place to vent anticipation, expectations, and angst about what often seems a daunting hurdle. Blogs, of course, have the added advantage of anonymity and the luxury of the privacy of the act of writing. Contributors can take their time creating their post or comment and can thoughtfully flesh out their ideas. Indeed many of the entries at 70Candles.com are lengthy and often very personal messages. As you'll see in the excerpts that follow, women have used this time to reflect on this landmark, review aspects of life thus far, try to derive meaning from their experiences, and peer into the future. The decade of the 70's marked a genuine turning point for many. Just listen!

From Anonymous, Age 70. *I'm waiting to feel the maturity and wisdom I've always assumed all the old ladies had.*

From Enid, age 70. *I haven't figured out yet what it means to be 70. It's just a number so far, but so loaded that I feel I ought to have some deep thoughts about it. I don't. I still feel like my usual self, and, although my hair has been grey for a long time, I am still surprised at times to see my reflection.*

As for being the oldest in a room, it really never occurs to me, although it is often true that I am. I find it just as easy to relate to every age as to any special one. In my own mind, I don't stand out as an old person, just one of the gang. It is astonishing to be offered a seat on the subway. I often feel like offering MY seat. This sometimes leads me to wonder if I should be 'acting my age,' whatever that might mean. I find the concept of aging confusing. I am glad to be around to experience it. It is with great difficulty that I connect the number 70 with the friends of my youth who, as Shakespeare said, are 'forever young.' I am a retired nurse, and for the last five years have been working as a model for art schools, a whole different world, and I love it.

From Frances, age 70. *I found the run-up to my 70th birthday quite sobering. Mild ailments that I customarily ignored seemed to portend serious conditions. Feeling sleepy suddenly seemed age-related. Thinking about purchasing clothing or household items made me wonder whether this was the last time I would be buying a new coat/blanket/tea kettle. Now that my birthday has passed, things seem to be returning to normal—thank goodness!*

The emotion that I find most helpful at this age is gratitude. I am grateful for good health, for the choices I have, for my family, for my friends, and for living in a place where I feel safe and free. When one feels grateful, it is impossible to feel angry. This realization has made a huge difference in my life. I try to turn anger around to gratitude—whether it's a disappointment, a frustration, or a sadness that is triggering the potential for anger, I try to think instead about something in that vein for which I can be grateful. Waiting in a line? I'm grateful that I have my iPhone to occupy me and take my mind off the 'wasted' time. Time is never wasted when you have an iPhone! Disappointment that one of my kids did something of which I disapprove? I'm grateful that they are their own people, with their own lives, making their own mistakes and successes, and that they are responsible for themselves. Of course, I lapse…I am human! But this paradigm shift has really helped me to let go of things I used to want to control, and to relax about being of an age where I am not expected to control a lot.

Of course, I sometimes feel marginalized. I feel invisible in some situations. Our generation is on the fringes now. I don't understand a lot of today's culture, technology, or humor. But it's okay—I have more time to process and enjoy the people and activities that bring me pleasure or challenge me in good ways. I'm ready to let it go and seek new ways to feel productive.

Giving myself permission not to be productive every minute of every day has been a huge freedom. It's okay to read in the middle of the day. I can spend an hour walking somewhere instead of finding the most efficient way to get from point A to point B. I can talk on the phone to a friend and not worry about what I'm not doing...most of the time! It's a work in progress, this evolution to being a retired 70-year-old. But it is progress! And I'm feeling so grateful to have the opportunity to do it.

Follow Your Bliss

From Marcia, Age 70. *About ten months prior to turning 70, I told my husband that I would like to celebrate my 70th birthday in Italy...Perhaps it was because 70 began to feel like I was really getting older, and that I wouldn't have forever to experience such a trip. ...Seventy is as vibrant an age as we make it out to be, given our state of health, but perhaps more importantly, our state of mind.*

I feel so alive from this experience, and also wonder where we might choose to go next in this wonderful world. Following our bliss at this point in our lives seems natural and important. What is your bliss at this time?

Seeking New Passions

From Tara, 69 and 6 months. *I recently stumbled upon your blog while surfing the Internet and am glad I found 70Candles, as I will be turning 70 in six months. I have been thinking how I want to celebrate this milestone and decided to plan a gift to myself. Even though I am married with two stepchildren and one grandson, I did not want to depend on them to do something. So last year I booked a walking trip of Tuscany to coincide with my special day. I will be celebrating in Italy with a younger girlfriend who shares a birthday around the same time.*

Turning 70 is not like turning 60. It sounds old to me even though I have heard that 70 is the new 50. Most of my friends are younger than I am, and luckily, I am blessed with good health so I can keep up with them physically and mentally. I am glad to serve as a role model for them as they age.

I recently retired from a 40+ year career as a physical therapist. As I move into a new decade, I am looking for a new passion to sustain me into my 70's.

Alive and Kicking!

From Sophia, Age 70. *I'm busy with not a moment to spare, but I still do the impossible, share all my time with lots of people daily. I care about politics, government issues at home, in the U.S., abroad, love to travel, like good food, good people, good times, good weather. Some of these things are free, others costly, one chooses. All this makes me feel alive and kicking!*

But, the day before my big birthday four days ago, I had a crisis. I didn't want to see or hear of anyone on my big day, nor did I want to burn any candles. I sent an email to my 12 most important people asking them not to notice me the following day. I was not going to be in the mood. I knew they were ready to celebrate my b-day, but I said I didn't want any mentioning of it. I shocked everyone with my out-of-character request and my negative and bitter message.

But 18 hours later, I brushed my email off, and I rebounded. My middle son lectured me on my email, rightly so; a friend said to me in a reprimanding email that I should be happy to be 70 and what was this nonsense of a 'crisis,' I should stop being silly. Little by little I became myself once more and laughed a lot on my birthday.

A friend just told me that what I wanted to forget had the opposite effect; we will all remember my 70th birthday with this anecdote and the tantrum I threw. Honestly, I feel the same at 70 years and four days—smart, witty, funny, courageous, picky, curious, crazy, etc. Life is a present, at 1, 64 or 90. ♪♫•* *just Let it Be, Let it Be* ♪♫•*. *Enjoy the ride, we have only one ticket!*

From Charlotte, Almost 70. *I'll celebrate my 70th birthday this month. I am planning to shamelessly exploit this milestone for my benefit. For the month of April and for the remains of the year I have committed to the thorough and thoughtful exploration of my hopes and dreams for my future. I wish to be no April fool, but yikes! It's hard to really sit myself down and convince me that this the "final third" or "final fourth" portion of life. I believe it's a sacred and essential exercise to take a deep look and let it sink in that this, at long last, is "it." Like so many I have spent so much of my life not recognizing the precious gifts of each day of my life as moments of "it." I want my dearest dreams and deepest hopes to surface clearly and fairly quickly, for at this wise age I really do realize how fast my life spins by. There is a sense of urgency—a certain sense I have lived not "too long" but "too short."*

There is a life to review and there is meaning to be made. I have important developmental work to do: a life to complete, and my life's legacy to tie up and deliver. Seventy is good from my perspective. Consider the alternative. I love a rainy day. I love the snow, the cold, the clouds, and the sunshine. Just take it all in! Keep moving, eat a healthy diet, and enjoy family, good company and great friends for as long as possible.

As we read through the blog entries we saw that many tended to fall into semi-discrete categories. We've grouped them here, as we will again in the chapter describing our in-person conversation groups. The blog-topics that emerged quite vividly (all seeming equally important, as judged by the number of times they were mentioned) are Work and Retirement, Ageism, Caretaking (the Club Sandwich Generation), Where to Live (Next), Grandparenting, Functional Changes, Social Connections, and the "Last Great Event" (Death). These classifications are not strictly independent of each other, but they proved to be a convenient way for us to view the material and allowed us to compare and contrast the views of different women.

We found in our blogs more stories of troubles, worries, illness, and pain than we heard in our later conversation groups. Beyond the angst of turning 70, stories also told of health struggles and financial and family crises. Some women were anxious about facing the end of their lives, especially if they were alone.

Perhaps because of the anonymity provided online, women who were lonely, sad, or suffering at this point in their lives felt free to ask for ideas or counsel from others. Conversely, we saw that our face-to-face gatherings, our conversation groups, were full of laughter, including laughing at ourselves. It is extremely interesting that the two vehicles we used to elicit women's experiences proved to have such dramatically different tones—each valid and reflective of our experiences. In both cases women were there to support each other, as you will see below in the gentle, encouraging responses from readers to many of the blog entries. They became a testament for us of the importance of sharing our 70 year-old lives—either in writing or in-person, and ideally both.

WORK AND RETIREMENT

Many women mentioned retirement, with lots of discussion about what to do with the ocean of time that seemed to open up when paid work ended. Or, just as significantly, what is the "right time," "if ever" as one woman put it, to retire. Or, what happens if your spouse retires, and you're not ready yet? The sub-themes are numerous. We want to share one particularly poignant post from a woman who unexpectedly and suddenly was fired and one of the responses it elicited. We also received many responses to queries about how to spend your time once you're retired. We'll share some of those responses, as well. Finally, you'll see one of several posts we received about financial concerns after retirement.

From Brenda, Age 70. *Thank you for throwing me your lifeline. The love of my life, my husband of 30 years, sent me your blog. He is 13 years my junior. I was blessed with good genes; I never ever admitted my age.*

From a vibrant, positive, superwoman turned 70, my life changed last November. I lost my job. I loved my career, helping people in need. It was a total shock. It was a blow to my ego. I felt that I was kicked to the curb.

My husband's career is in a home office. I seem to always be irritating him, even though I'm seldom home. I volunteer at a Sharing Center, with homeless people, etc., but I am very unhappy with life. My career, which I loved, dominated my life. I am now available to friends and loved ones, but I am having a mental crisis. I know the problem is ME.

Response from Ellen:

I have read your post several times, and I find it very moving. Thank you for being so honest. 70Candles is an opportunity for us to share our REAL lives, the challenges and the joys. I am so sorry you lost your job. I can relate to that. I was a full professor when I moved three years ago (at age 69) and did not even get an interview for two Assistant Professor jobs I applied for. I was devastated. When you say "the problem is ME," I don't buy that. You lost your job. That is awful. However, it sounds to me as though the SOLUTION may be you. What can you do that would be meaningful to you? You are a good writer. You loved helping people in need. Good, these are clues to next steps. You say you're unhappy with your life. Is there something even small that makes you happy? Do it more. And keep sharing, as you've done here. One thing I've learned from reading 70Candles is that talking to each other about what's important to us is VERY important. Good luck to you, and thank you for writing.

Response from Miriam:

The identities and roles people hold when they are employed can really influence how they feel about themselves in and out of the office. It can be tough and even devastating to find new ways to continue feeling productive once you stop working. It sounds like you've found ways to feel intellectually and emotionally productive, which is great! I wonder if there are new activities that you and your husband can do together that might be fulfilling for both of you—volunteering, taking up a new hobby, sharing teaching experiences (you teach him something you know how to do, he teaches you something that he feels skilled in).

Response from Rita:

Reading your blog brought memories of myself at that stage ten years ago—I chose to leave work planning to move into a life of creativity and freedom—even though I had loved my work. Instead I found myself drowning in emptiness, a loss of identity and structure, loss of purpose and the daily companionship of like-minded people. I couldn't bear the sight of my partner happily working at things he enjoys. It is a huge loss. Allow yourself to grieve. Take time to find yourself in this new stage of life. May I offer a few points?

- *avoid immersing yourself in kitchen and housework—it will make you very resentful!*

- *don't rush into too many volunteer activities, or you will find yourself being 'busy' doing things you don't particularly enjoy and feeling too guilty to drop out.*

- *create an office/studio/workspace for yourself where you can close the door and meditate/read books/listen to music, work at whatever you want.*

- *investigate blogs and blogging—a marvelous source for meeting like-minded people.*

Do keep us posted on your progress. This is a splendid stage of life, but like everything else it has to be worked at and created. Enjoy the process.

Response from Tanya:

I, too, am asked what I do with all this spare time. I taught young children for years. I loved doing that but found it an emptying process. Now I am refilling my cup of life. Instead of racing here and there to beat a clock or traffic, I sit. I listen. I become a part of the landscape. I simply take time for myself. How else can we get to know who we are? Time is on our side...it goes faster as you get older...make it your time.

Yes, to the 64 year old blogger, it is good to have time to find yourself in your new life. In fact, I think it is necessary to pause before feeling you must DO something. I retired two years ago and moved from New York City to Cape Cod. I had a period of culture shock. I had several interests I now have time to pursue more diligently, but I did not rush to make new acquaintances and a place in my new community. It has evolved more quickly than I expected, but I still feel I'm taking my time—and I have the time. I love getting up every morning with the knowledge that I can fill the day with my interests. I'm feeling more creative than I have in years. So taking your time seems like exactly the right thing for you to do.

Tough Times, But a Reality for Some

From Iris, Age 70. *This September I will be 70, a fearsome age that somehow I never seriously considered. Compared to many women of my age, I am doing well. I am married, my second husband is a good companion, I am in fair health, and we have barely enough money to last the rest of our lives. I retired at 65 and thought I would have a fairly comfortable rest-of-my-life.*

Money is the big issue, so my dreams have bit the dust. No more foreign trips, which we had done often when we were both working, no more jumping on a plane to go see our only daughter who lives across the country, and living in a state of constant frugality and fear of spending even a few dollars for a movie because we may need it to live on our 80's and, god forbid, our 90's. I have also had to give up any charitable or political or religious giving. I have squeezed out a small amount for our church yearly, but it is nowhere near the amount we used to give. I have completely cut off charitable giving to anything but the church. That makes me feel guilty and like a failure, but it is the reality. Our biggest expenditures for the rest of our lives are going to be health insurance and health coverage. That's a grim future without much lightness or joy or hope.

So here I am...almost 70, knocked out of the upper class to the middle class and now to below-the-poverty-line class, focusing on making do, reusing, doing without, in order to keep as much money as possible for health insurance and health care. Certainly not where I ever thought I would be.

AGEISM

These posts speak for themselves. There is much written about ageism, a still pervasive problem. Here is what our readers have to say.

From Harriet, Age 70. *I recall the moment when I realized that I had passed some "age" bar in the minds of others. I was in the hospital having carpal tunnel surgery because I could no longer swim or bike comfortably. Before surgery, a young intern came to interview me. One of his questions was how much I walked. I said two miles a day was my minimum. He could not hear "miles." He wrote "two blocks." That was my first bump with age prejudice.*

Terms of Endearment

From Anonymous, Age 70. *Often I call my 7 year old granddaughter "Sweet Girl" and my husband "Hon." I'm used to terms of endearment of a certain kind…but something is changing. Lately, people have caught me off guard.*

My handsome, gay, male masseuse finished my last session with "OK, Cupcake!" And the receptionist at my doctor's office closed a phone conversation with "OK, Sweet Girl!" Both left me perplexed, as I recoiled. What impression am I leaving, I wonder, with these very pleasant, well-intended adults? They certainly don't mean to be patronizing.

I still feel like my mature, intellectually intact self. Am I looking or sounding childlike? Are they so aware of my age that they are feeling kindly…nurturing…maybe relating to me with feelings they have for their own grandparents?

I wonder…Is this happening to you?

Snubbing Ageism

From Sheila, Almost 70. *I believe it is foolish to listen to our culture's standard language and lore of aging and ageism. I refuse to believe the "it's all downhill from here" messages that I hear so frequently from friends, family members, and even talkative strangers in the checkout lines at our local grocery stores. I will admit to some obvious signs of physical change; for instance my eyebrows have lately gone wildly weird. And the pesky black hairs on my face have turned white, but they are still pesky. To top it all off I have no idea what my actual hair color is because it has been "highlighted" and "lowlighted" for so long, a common camouflage technique for women of my age. Physically, I do not consciously feel a whole lot different than I remember feeling at 40. Perhaps I have a memory system that has softened the edges of the results of gradual physical changes, but I'll take this kind and fuzzy memory of physical decline.*

Confessing Ageism

From Abby, Age 29. *OK my confession. I must thank you for your inspiration, however I must admit I am nowhere near the wisdom levels that you have achieved.*

I have come across this site by a stroke of luck or just divine intervention. I am a second year college student. At the request of my Gerontology Professor, I am required to write a paper on imagining my self at 70 years of age. I have been reading through the stories, and I find myself, laughing at the variety of life experiences you have all had. However, I also find my self feeling ashamed, for the assignment I just completed for College, I made the 8th decade age group seem like lifeless dolls, collecting dust on a shelf.

I am sorry to say but, I have just written a 13 page paper on the idea of what I envision my life to be like when I turn 70 years old. The medical break down of everything imaginable that I fear will be wrong with me. The fact that I wrote an entire paper on being 'too old' to do anything. I envisioned that I will sit on a swing, and pet my dog who would love a nice walk. He will never see one because I would be too sore, to take him, the fact that I will watch my great grandchildren from a chair because my bones will ache too much to play.

I must apologize for my ageism. But I fear that I really had no idea what I was writing about. It is interesting to think that I was able to write a paper about something that I obviously know nothing about.

I was concerned about my 30th Birthday coming up next month. But I suppose you would be the wrong group to complain about that to.

Thank you for this new information that I have found and the inspiration to know that my time is far from over, and there is no need to assume that just because we are told life is short does not mean it is over already.

Response from Ellen:

Thank you, Abby, for your fabulous post. And BTW, I hated turning 30. It symbolized for me responsibility, ugh. I told everyone I knew to ignore my birthday, and of course when they did I was even more heartsick. When I turned 70 my family gathered together in Lake Placid and we went snowshoeing. I wish you could send your post to every 29 year old in the world. I love how honest you are. But don't be disappointed with yourself for not knowing better…how could you!! Ageism is everywhere. When someone says something like "she's 70 years young" they think they are being cute and flattering. I want to scream, "70 is old, and that's okay." Developmental psychologists tell us that every stage and phase of life has its rewards and challenges, but vibrancy needn't fade away as long as we're alive. You have added so much to this blog site. Thank you!!

CARETAKING—THE CLUB SANDWICH GENERATION

Caretaking can take its toll on women, especially if they have little or no support system in place for themselves. As they are often sandwiched between parents, grown children, and at times grandchildren, any of whom might need their care, we refer to these caregivers as "The Club Sandwich Generation." We heard from some women who sounded quite discouraged and some rather desperate. We and our bloggers tried to lend support with counsel and kind encouragement.

Finding it Hard

From Maria, Age 73. *I am 73 years old and find it hard to come to terms with getting old. I miss my youth, the attention span, the energy I had, and having something to look forward to. Now my time is spent caring for my husband who has changed so much that I don't know him. We have three* *children and eight adult grandchildren, but the caretaking is up to me. Sorry to be so negative but this is how I feel.*

Response from Ellen:

It has to be terribly hard to take care of an ailing husband, especially one who has changed so much. I've never had to deal with that, so have not walked in our shoes, but please try to think of something that could possibly change in the future to bring some joy to your life. With the family members, couldn't someone take care of your husband for a short while, so you could have a break? We all need something to look forward to, even if it is a small trip or visit with someone from long ago. There has to be some good in your life; try to concentrate on that and let the past go. We can never get back to the way we were, as much as we might want to.

Response from Vickie:

Maria, the most important thing I've learned in my lifetime is that life can be tough. To deny that is preposterous. I feel for you. I can only imagine what it must be like to be a caretaker for an ailing husband who you don't know anymore. Thank you for sharing this. By reaching out you've invited in a lot of compassion, and we all benefit from that kind of sharing. But I also know something about the value of being kind to others, feeling and expressing gratitude, figuring out what our strengths are and using these strengths every day. If you are, for example, a curious person, discover one new thing a day. I appreciate you for expressing what you call your negativity, but I would also want to hear what's meaningful to you, what brings you joy, when you feel at your best. Because I know that's there too.

From Anonymous, age 69. *I turn 70 next month. You talk about flourishing, while I'm feeling rather trapped instead.*

I'm caring for my 90 year-old mother who needs help with everything. My brother is willing to contribute financially, but he says he's not comfortable ministering to Mom's personal needs. How are other women dealing with these issues? So many of our parents are living into their nineties and even beyond. I need advice and some help!

FUTURE LIVING ARRANGEMENTS

In addition to the problems and benefits derived from membership in the Club Sandwich generation, there was a lively conversation in the blogosphere about the decision to stay put or move to senior friendly living quarters. Many wrestled with the challenge of moving at this age and fear of the unknown. Responses to women trying to make this major life decision were wise and empathic.

Fear of the Unknown

This fairly long entry contains themes and feelings about housing that were expressed by many. The topic clearly struck a chord, as demonstrated by a large number of responses from readers, a few of which we include below.

From Claire, Almost 70. *I will reach the ripe old age of 70 on March 22, which is already lightly knocking on my door. I am an only child who has had no natural children. I'm retired and live alone. My foster son lives three and a half hours away. He is encouraging me to move closer to him so I will have someone to check on me and someone to give me support when needed. I went riding around and found a house for sale that I kinda liked. I've collected antiques for years, and my furniture could really be show-cased in this house.*

I actually became excited about the house and it's been one of the few things I've been excited about in a very long time.

I admit I've gotten into quite a rut here. I actually don't have any really close friends here. I worked in the neighboring town for 30 years and my job was my life. After I retired, I realized how few people I really knew here.

I haven't bought the house but was getting very close to making an offer. It's all become overwhelming and terribly so. I have accumulated tons of stuff at this house after 39 years; that, coupled with being a pack rat. I work one day on trying to go through things and the next day I can hardly walk due to my ankle. So it goes.

This weekend I am getting cold feet and lots of doubts are creeping in. The only view from the "new" house is one of the ugliest houses I've ever seen which is across the street. On a positive note, if I moved, I would have a son, daughter-in-law, and three grandchildren checking in on me and would have loads of activities to keep me involved. I would also have a job waiting for me, a sit-down job, with one of my son's friends. I would have a ready-made set of friends through my son's family and I absolutely love the church they go to.

I'm scared to death!! What if I move and am miserable and all I can think about is the place I've left with the beautiful view. What if I'm not happy there? On the other hand, I'm not exactly happy here either, just comfortable. I realize happiness is not a place; it's a state of mind, or at least that's what I've always been told. I really don't know what my true feelings are. I've been on a roller coaster for days—one minute semi-excited about the house and displaying my antiques, and then I think about looking out the window at that gosh-awful ugly house across the street. The next minute I feel so overwhelmed that I literally think a move is virtually impossible.

Surely I am not the only 70-year old (or almost) to experience such conflicting feelings. Many older people, including my parents, have been faced with the difficult decision of uprooting themselves or being uprooted by relatives as a necessity. Reality tells me that I do need to be closer to people who care about me…

How do I conquer the "fear of the unknown?" I'm in such a quandary now that I honestly don't know what I feel about anything. I have all these thoughts swirling through my mind. If I were young, I could move, knowing I could always move back if I wasn't happy. But, I'm not young; I'm older than dirt!! And, I only want to make one move—if any, at all.

The house is darling, with a front porch and a back porch, which I've always loved. It has the conveniences I need and will have to have at some point in time if I live long enough.

What do you think? Do I do something that I'm not totally convinced that I want to do because it seems the most intelligent thing to do, or do I remain comfortable, always wondering what it would have been like and knowing at the same time that a move is inevitable—maybe not now, but definitely in the future...

I would love to hear what others think about the situation, but, unfortunately, I need answers quickly. The offer needs to be done this week or I stand to lose the opportunity of getting this particular house, and should I move, I really think this particular house was in many ways made for me—even with the ugly house across the street. Ha! Thanks for listening.

Response from Georgia:

Go. Enjoy the adventure. There isn't much in life that is truly written in stone, so take the chance. Remember if it doesn't work out for you, you can always make another decision. At 66 I moved from where I had lived for nearly 25 years to a state 1,000 miles away; I was alone, I didn't have a job, and I didn't know anyone. The challenge has invigorated me in ways I could not have imagined and enriched my life in the process.

Go through your house and give away some of the things to people you care for where you live now; give things to charities knowing that somewhere, someone will treasure them and put them to good use. Take the things you love and want around you and enjoy your wonderful foster son and family and your new job. This is a new and wonderful opportunity for you—leap into it with all your might. Love and luck.

Response from Anna:

A couple of things. At 70 I moved from Orcas Island in the Pacific Northwest to Taos, New Mexico. I am an only child; I have an only child, my daughter, who lives in the SF Bay area. She comes to visit a couple of times a year. It was a great move. I've been here eight years and I've made new friends, I'm living in one of the most beautiful places on the planet, and in spite of health issues, I'm doing fine. I strongly urge you to buy a house on one level (after 75, arthritis really kicked in!) and to divest yourself of any possessions that you don't love, find beautiful, or find to be useful. I gave away more than half of what I owned and I don't miss it a bit! Say yes to a new life— reinvent yourself! May your life be rich and full of days,

Response from Leslie:

Sounds like it's 50/50, equally divided between good and bad! A difficult choice, but for me, being around family— not so they can look after me, although that's implied, but so I can revel in their closeness—would be decisive. It sounds like you can do everything there (and more) that you are doing in the current situation. So I agree, the only really bad challenge is the fear, the change, the transition. But you might consider this: what if in five or ten years you want to move but then you're REALLY scared, and now you have less money because you've been frittering it away due to boredom (and what does that tell you?). You are so lucky to have caring family. Best wishes!

Response from Ruth:

I wonder if there is a way to move but leave an option open to return, like not selling your present house. My instinct is to go, to embrace the new opportunity, perhaps find a different house with a better view that you like more. I moved 12 years ago for similar reasons and was scared to death of not knowing anyone in the new community. I've found that my interests—gardening, horses, animals, the outdoors—have been gateways to new friends. I love that you would have your own space and independence. You sound like an interesting person, but it is normal isn't it to fear the unknown? I certainly did and still do. Good luck!

Response from Paula:

Good morning! You do have some big decisions to make, that's for sure. The one thing that stands out to me is that if you do decide to move closer to your son and his family, you still need to find ways to create a new life for yourself. I have seen it happen so often where the parent moves to be closer to their son/daughter and they are working, have their own friends, activities, etc. I am 77 and have re-created my life several times with various moves starting with my divorce 41 years ago.

I do agree that a house on one level is very important. Also, if you don't like the "view" from the house you are looking at, you will "hate" it once you are moved in. I know that, too, as I moved into this independent senior apartment complex seven and a half years ago. Before I have always had my own outdoor space: patio, balcony, etc. Here I don't. I thought I could handle it, but I hate not having that. Good luck on your decisions.

Not a Rose Garden

From Beatrice, Age 71. *I have been divorced since age 49, and have always been blessed with good looks. I feel I wasted years in a bad marriage, but had two sons and a fear of being alone. My son decided to join the Israeli army, and I planned to follow him. I did this and loved it. I loved the country and, fearful of the transition of returning to the U.K., I stayed and bought a beautiful penthouse. When I was 69 (and feeling very young), property prices dropped in the U.K. Here was my chance to sell the penthouse and stay with my kids in the U.K. I bought a large apartment [fully decorated]. After two months, such loneliness! I felt so cold, externally and internally, that I then decided I would have to return to Tel-Aviv. Meanwhile, apartments in Tel-Aviv had risen 27%, and the pound sterling had dropped to an historical low, so I decided to rent my apartment in London, and live in two rooms in Tel-Aviv.*

I ask myself now, does anything really matter? I don't want to recognize my age. Yes, I have grandchildren, and I love them, but this alone is not a life. Turning 70 is frightening when you're alone. I wish I were richer. Even phone calls from friends are all health complaints. This is not a rose garden. I am healthy, still look good, but tell me there's something more than this! PLEASE!

Response from Sandy:

When you ask if anything really matters, I wonder if what you're talking about is where you live. It sounds like there are advantages and disadvantages to Tel Aviv and London, so maybe that's what doesn't really matter. You— and I—can create a life wherever we happen to be. Just a thought.

GRANDPARENTING

Many women mentioned their grandchildren in their blog posts. Some of the grandkids were close-by, others at a distance. There were regrets that they were so far away, eagerness to know them better, and for others, a bit of fatigue at being "on-demand." Some, like the blogger above, said that being a grandma was in itself not a life. Others believed their grandchildren were their lives at this age.

From Faye, Age 76. *It`s been six years since I tried to blow out all 70 candles. And though my neck sags, and I can`t remember my neighbor`s name, though I need hearing aids and depend upon Depends, these most recent years have brought a kind of ecstasy that make such indignities mere inconveniences. After a long delay impatiently awaiting the arrival of grandchildren, I`ve recently been blessed with two winsome grandsons who have made these years more glorious than my most extravagant imaginings.*

Though I have trouble getting up after a floor game with our three year old, and I keep the shape of a chair when I rise, this phase of life has been a gathering of fruits nurtured over many years. While I anticipated reliving the joys of raising my children through theirs, I had not foreseen the sheer joy of seeing my son as parent to his son.

A parallel process has taken place in my career. Though I am addled by the challenges of new technology, and my clinical field has changed dramatically, I enjoy the cumulative experience of many active years in the field and the pleasure of continued contact with generations of students I supervised over more than three decades. Like so much of life, the 70s have brought challenges and losses, blessings and unexpected reward.

Response from Doris:

I am 75 and have been a grandmother since I was 36! Married very young (as was my daughter), I had 4 children, 7 grandchildren and now am the very proud great grandmother of 8! I can identify with what you said. Seeing my children as grandparents is so amazingly wonderful. Holding a great grandchild and seeing their parents and grandparents in them is thrilling! I have been so very blessed and I try to just keep on keeping on! I have some physical challenges but I try to just keep going (like the Eveready bunny. Thanks for reminding me of the joys of family...and the many reasons we have to keep going.

FUNCTIONAL CHANGES

Women wrote about hearing loss, aches and pains, unidentified ailments, joint replacements, general slowing down, and fear of future physical and mental decline. The literature of course strongly supports the importance of staying active, and this cannot be overemphasized in this or any other publication.

From Terry, Age 69. *I'm turning 70 next year, and it's a little scary to think my life is coming to an end. After the 60s it's all downhill from there. I never married or had children. My parents are deceased and I have one brother in Arizona living in a resort. I retired at 62 and keep busy at home. I worked very hard for 45 years, and now I'm resting a lot (ha). I have many friends and go out to eat often. I talk with one each day to keep my sanity (ha).*

I'm not afraid to die, just how it happens matters. I'm not sure I want to be 80 or older. Too many ailments. I think I'll just forget about birthdays from now on and just focus on living a good life.

From Gloria, Age 69. *I am quickly looking at age 70 and I am having a difficult time of it. I know it is just a number... or so I tell myself...but the truth is I feel like it is my first step onto the death train.*

Yes, I know we are all going to die, but this age is downright traumatic for me. I had a heart attack a little over a year ago, and was lucky to survive. It kicked in thyroid issues, and now a few weeks ago I took radioactive iodine to slow down/ kill my thyroid. Now I have limited energy. My hair also got thin and brittle.

Before this, I was performing music regularly, writing, going to a lot of parties, doing crafts, etc. Now it all seems meaningless.

I am still fairly attractive and force myself to work out, be somewhat social, etc...but force is the operative word here. I have no husband, boyfriend, or children. I have always had a lot of friends, but my energy there is diminishing.

I am not suicidal...but turning 70 had totally messed with my head. I can't take anti-depressants because of the reaction to meds I am taking. So, what now?

Response from Ellen:

I had a cortisone shot for my hip today and was told I have the early stages of degenerative joint disease (osteoarthritis). I have walked marathons, played tennis avidly, and considered myself a woman who "loved/ lived to sweat." I've joked that's what would appear on my tombstone. Now that's not the same as a heart attack, and my hair remains thick and curly; I'm making only the smallest of comparisons. I'm so sorry you've had to suffer these hardships. But we do have this in common: We are not what we used to be. I often think of that old bumper sticker, "Old Age is Not for Sissies." And we're only APPROACHING old age at 70-ish.

I'm wondering what you might do to adapt and even thrive in what may not be our golden years, but certainly are important years of our lives. One book I suggest for you is called "The Resilience Factor: 7 Essential Skills for Overcoming Life's Inevitable Obstacles" by Karen Reivich and Andrew Shatte. It's not about aging—in fact I recently recommended it to a high school football player who was being recruited by an Ivy League university until he had a game-ending injury. Yet I found it helpful as I prepared for my cortisone shot, today. Look particularly at a concept the authors call Real-time Resilience. The theme is that you can change the way you THINK about your life.

SOCIAL CONNECTIONS

Above all, the importance of connection with others jumped out from both the blog postings and the conversation groups as particularly salient for our 70Candles women. When our respondents were lonely, they suffered in myriad ways. Reaching out to others might just be the #1 prescription for a satisfying, flourishing eighth decade.

From Loretta, Age 72. *Generally, this is a fine and liberating time of life, enhanced by the great richness of friendship with women (most of them over many decades), the freedom to pursue pleasure far more than duty, and the delight I our grown children and grandchildren and our wisely aging parents.*

From Irene, Age 70. *I began my turn at 69 though I did not know it at the time it was happening. And for nearly two years now I have been browsing over my experiences living from childhood to now, trying to understand on a very deep level the choices I made, what I have done and how I got here. It is almost as if I am rebuilding my foundation. I began autobiographical writing, and then stories based on my experiences, started looking for my long lost meaningful* *friends. I became a self-published author and archived all my writings. That was hard enough but the hardest part was watching the women my own age timing themselves out and settling, while I feel I am just getting warmed up.*

Suddenly I realized that I don't fit into the society immediately around me, and I accept that as part of my new life path. I had to stop doing what no longer serves me and distance myself from the negative influences of those aging around me who are not optimistic, living out their same story, only talking about medications, doctors, pains and getting old. With those people out of my social life now I find myself wondering where my tribe is, who my people are. I spend a lot of time alone, writing, reading and loving it. It is better than the alternative of trying to relate to negativity and patronization about age. I look forward to what will be new and wonderful, what will move my heart and what will bring tears of joy to my eyes. I have no time for sorrow about getting older. I am merely doing it and trying to love it deeply as I go.

Bumps in the Road

From Judy, Age 69. *I stumbled onto this website in my search for, what? I don't know. I just turned 69 in November, and the first birthday that has traumatized me. I am having the worst time with it, but reading some of the stories has helped me realize that I am not losing my mind. What I am experiencing is normal, or at least for some of us.*

Two of my dearest friends have moved away. One across country, the other a day away. This has really left a gap in my life. Just a few years ago my life was so very different. I have been widowed for 20 yrs. and was content with just my friends, my social life. Now I am feeling such a void. My grandchildren who played a big part in my life are teenagers, and I am not as important to them. My own mother passed away last year as did my only sister a few yrs. ago.

Maybe I need a kick in the butt to stop the self-pity. Hope so cause this is not what I want out of the rest of my life. I intend to keep on with this site and try and be more positive. Thanks for listening!

Response from Linda:

I hope that by now you are starting to wake up and face the inevitable: we age, we have history (as you point out), but each day brings us a fresh opportunity to enjoy the natural world, good food, music, movies, other people. My only warning is: don't worry about the bad stuff in the world, avoid romantic movies, stop taking walks down memory lane. Instead: please clean out your closets, get rid of stuff you don't use, if you can afford it go on an elder hostel trip, or study Spanish in Mexico in one of the lovely colonial cities such as San Miguel de Allende or Oaxaca. Volunteer reading at your local elementary school, help out in an animal shelter—get outside of yourself. I'm 70 and trying to see my life in a positive way, for one, being grateful for what I have, accepting the fact that I am responsible for my own happiness. Be strong. Stay cool. All the best.

Response from Susan:

You are definitely not alone. I am facing 70 in May and totally freaked out about it. It is messing with my perspective on life. I used to be life of the party, go to a lot of parties, perform music, and be up for any adventure. I went to Paris on my own last summer. Now I feel like I am getting too old to do anything. I have no husband, boyfriend, or children. I just don't feel like there is life...a sense of wonder...a possibility of finding a mate...or much of anything in my future. Maybe things will change, but this is where I am right now. So, again, you are not alone!

Response from Karen:

I'm having the exact same experience. I am so used to being 'young,' I don't quite know how to handle this "about to turn 70 thing!" Hard to enjoy being in your late 60's...for the 'scary fact of being old,' and yes, 70 sounds "Old" to me, so did 60! I'm trying to adapt, not doing too well with it though. My husband died long ago, at only age 46. I married again, but way too soon, and realized that I was then searching "for what I had." It could have worked had I been able to give it a chance, but although I wanted that kind of happiness again, I destroyed its chances. And now...sigh. I wish "I had put the past behind me and made it work." And now...I just don't know. I look young still, but am not willing to go looking, and wouldn't begin now to know where to look for "Happiness Again." So, I feel as though I'm just "drifting" through life now...the kind of Happiness I want, I suppose is gone forever...so see..."You're not Alone"!

Reconnecting with Old Friends

From Dottie, Age 78. *In anticipation dread of retirement to begin this August, I have initiated email correspondence with one special friend from each segment of my life, of which there were three—hence three gals, HS, College, Grad School, after decades of drifting apart. It has been an unexpected joy for them and for me.*

ADDITIONAL PERSPECTIVES

One reader started a conversation about death that elicited many responses. This is a topic we had not anticipated, but one that we now understand has profound importance for our generation.

From Peggy, Age 62. *Working on my Retirement Project I came across "70Candles" and was immediately drawn in, especially by the phrase, "The baby boomers are fast on our heels, and want to know what lies ahead." I'm one of those Baby Boomers, and I have become absolutely fascinated with how we, individually and culturally, respond to aging. Recently retired, age 62, from my final employment career as an RN. I received my B.S. in Nursing at age 55, and have a B.A. in Biology and a M.A. in Theology. I only mention these because they, also have important roles in my world view.*

During the last 5 years I worked as a Visiting Nurse in an upstate NY college town. It wasn't the kind of nursing I thought I'd be doing but I fell in love. I experienced the incredible privilege to be present with patients, and their families and friends, through the process of long- or short-term illnesses, inevitable decline, and death. I have suffered with them through very hard decisions. I have comforted, advocated for, and rejoiced with as well. We were also managing health and decline.

It was this experience that inspired my Retirement Project, and it is this blog that inspired me to write this note. I want to help people be better prepared for, and more thoughtful about, the ramifications of the process of aging and inevitable decline. What can we reasonably expect? And how might our responses and choices affect our families, friends, and/or society?

The bottom line is that we, as a culture, continue to fear dying. Yet, in spite of the vast resources available, including Living Wills, Advanced Directives, Palliative Care, and Hospice, only a very small percentage of our population uses even these. We may even have Wills, and Life Insurance but we don't usually talk about it until there is no other choice. The saddest part is that we have turned the process of dying & death into the most negative thing in our lives, rather than seeing and experiencing it as a wondrous thing to behold. We prepare for births by learning about the process, we go through the process with some reasonable understanding of what to expect, and we celebrate the outcome—the first great event of a person's life. Should we do no less for the last great event of a person's life?

I know that this blogspot is dedicated to "Flourishing" and few people might relate talking about the process of decline as an example of "Flourishing," but I think we have a big opportunity. That's why I'm reaching out to my sisters engaged in "this Longevity Revolution." Because if this is "the revolution" what will it look like when so many more Baby Boomers are 70+?

So I've been taking informal surveys and pondering about how I can develop this Retirement Project idea. You have a lot of wisdom and experience among you and I'd love to hear your thoughts and opinions.

Response from Sylvia:

What an amazing project you have started. I am looking forward to what you Baby Boomers can teach us and the things that you will continue to change. I am 78 (next month) and in pretty good health and I try to keep a positive attitude about life. I consider myself a life-long learner. I have retired twice! You are right, though, we don't talk about dying. It's imperative that I get all my papers taken care of. My grown son (only child) moved to AZ a few months ago, and now I'm not sure how to get him Power of Attorney, etc. I plan to visit him mid-October. Keep up the good work. If you have ideas or suggestions for me, please let me know. Thanks again!

Response from Tara:

Right on! I heartily agree with your thoughts about embracing rather than fearing the last chapter in our lives. I am a retired physical therapist turning 70 this year. I have seen many "good" and "bad" deaths.

My hope is that the baby boomers will take on this challenge and change the paradigm about dying.

Response from Enid:

I am in Walton, Delaware County for what I think of as the four summer months. During that time, I, also a retired nurse, work as a hospice volunteer, and find it enriching to a degree I wouldn't have expected. I am also a member of a very tight-knit group of nursing graduates from Hartwick College in Oneonta, N.Y. Although we started with zeroing on to jobs, marriages, kids, we have gone, over the half century we've been getting together, to death of parents, the wonder of grandkids, deaths of spouses and each other. In facing all these things straight on, we have become strong and honest and of huge support to each other. People of the wider community would benefit enormously from these sorts of discussions about death as a part of life. Sounds like you're on the right track. I would love to be in touch with you.

Finally, a section unique to the blog, as we heard from women older and younger, who offered both poetry and prose in their views on life at different ages. We are delighted by these entries.

Written at age 18, in 1928
I'd Like to Know
By Dora V. Gordon

I often wonder what I'll be
At the age of seventy

Old and bent and doubled in two
Knitting as old ladies do

Sitting by the fireside
A woolen shawl around me tied

Wiping teardrops from my eye
As I think of days gone by?

Or dancing grandma will I be
With hennaed locks and painted knee

Newest steps and latest slang
Cocktail parties with the gang

Poiret frocks and high-heeled shoes
Strolling down the avenues?

Or in my grave will I have lain
Buried after much, much pain

And my tombstone will it state
I had a rendezvous with Fate

A victim of a heart disease
God bless me—may I rest in peace?

It worries me—this what I'll be
When I arrive at seventy.

Written at age 77, in 1987
And Now I Know
By Dora V. Gordon

Now I've reached that golden age
And every day I turn the page
To see what life is really like
Oh! It's different to say the least
I'll tell you this—it's quite a feast!

I'm not knitting by the fireside
There is no shawl around me tied
No time to think of days gone by
No time for all those pains and aches
It's run, run, run—for Heaven's sakes.

Things to do there always are
I sure keep going in that car
Whoever thought I'd come to this
Seventy plus and such fast gait
Always hopin' I won't be late

I'm on the run with this and that
I manage time like an acrobat
There's always much to see and do
Can't miss a thing, so off I go
And who has time to knit and sew?

Something new is always there
For us to learn about and care
Travel talks, trips and classes too
TV shows and parties great
Keeping fit—I'll just rejuvenate!

So that's the senior life, my friend
It's really like a dividend
Never thought it—way back when
So live it up—and take it in
Enjoying life is not a sin!

From Maggy Simony.

I'm 95 as of March 14th and remember Turning 70 as the ONLY decade birthday that bothered me.

I remember early 30s and 40s as the best time of my life. 40th and 50th birthdays? Not traumatic. By 50, I'd found a job that suited me to a T—secretary to the local high school principal. I was able to negotiate it down to a 10-month job, getting same time off as the teachers.

Turning 50, I was heading into troubled waters but unaware—my husband became ill and died at age 54. That decade moving into my 60s was difficult—widowed, with children married or off to college.

60th birthday I celebrated by retiring (one can retire as a widow at 60 with same social security terms as 62 if not a widow). And I wanted OUT of working. I was MADE to be retired "with interests" and time, time, time to pursue them. It was a foolish financial decision but right for me.

I almost absentmindedly drifted into finding the part-time work that would make the rest of my life interesting and fulfilling—self-publishing. And it got me out of my depression.

I bought an IBM Electronic Selectric machine. Learned book-page typesetting and set out to not only write and publish my first book, but typeset books for other small publishers and a magazine.

I knew there needed to be a compiled book of reading lists for travelers. I also knew no major publisher would publish such a book from someone like me without any professional credentials in compiling a bibliography. And so while pursuing a correspondence course with the University of Wisconsin, "Writing the non-fiction book," I came up with a good title: Traveler's Reading Guide—Ready-made Reading Lists for the Armchair Traveler—I produced and published three paperbacks over the years.

Turning 70 in 1990 WAS a bit of a Waterloo for me—malaise

and feeling I'd really entered old age now. A couple, long-time friends, who were taking a trip to Yugoslavia asked me to join them—added plus, no extra charge for singles—spend that dreaded birthday in Dubrovnik. I did, and spent my actual birthday on a day-trip cruise out of Dubrovnik with entire dining room singing happy birthday to me in Yugoslavian, and drinking champagne with my friends. By the time I got home I was over that temporary depression and have just been philosophical about aging since.

By this time I'd also gotten hooked at the library on another idea for a book that didn't exist—a book about playing sociable bridge. There are hundreds, thousands of books about serious bridge playing, not one I could find on sociable bridge even though sociable bridge players outnumber the serious players by the millions.

For reasons of procrastination, and I get feeling I'll live forever, I never did get around to publishing that bridge book until the end of 2009, at 89, with the title Bridge Table or What's Trump Anyway? An affectionate look back at sociable bridge & ladies lunch. By this time self-publishing had become widespread, far easier than back when I started. BUT one still must do the harder less fun job of marketing yourself. And so I started a blog, http://bridgetable.net as part of a rather desultory effort at marketing.

Meanwhile I moved to retirement heaven in Florida near a daughter. I'm still a political junkie, play bridge at least twice a week—and blog.

If people ask how come I do so well at 94 I emphasize the mental aspect. I do walk a bit, but I loathe sports—always have—and I don't even take my vitamins as I should. I believe mental activity is at least as important as physical activity—perhaps more important. I do watch to see that I eat enough protein and greens, but don't deny myself fried foods or yummy desserts when I eat out.

And I usually add—just for a laugh—have a martini every

night and go barefooted as much as possible. [I kind of believe in that Asian stuff about all those nerve endings in the soles of one's feet needing to be massaged by going barefooted or at least wearing thin-soled shoes.]

Just a couple months ago on 60 Minutes they did a piece on nonagenarians and what they have in common—came down to being slightly overweight and having a couple of drinks every day! I fit that.

My unscientific opinion is that heredity probably has more to do with reaching the 90s dementia-free than seems fair. But being mentally active is next—interested in life and the world, open to taking up new hobbies and activities that bring you in touch with a new set of acquaintances and friends. And, one thing more, learn to play bridge as early in life as you can. But it's never too late—take it up in your 70s for sure if you've reached 70 without bridge!

What's so unique about bridge? It's a classy, classic game that's been played in one form or other for hundreds of years. The whist of Jane Austen novels is the bridge of that day. Bridge is global. It's cheap to pursue if you wish. It never bores, guarantees you social contacts long after old friends and much of your family have died off. You can play literally to the end of life—sociably or seriously—despite arthritic fingers that bar crafts (get a card holder), loss of vision as long as you can see enlarged numbers and differentiate the suits, and hearing—people can yell during the bidding phase or hold up bid cards. Once bidding is over, you don't NEED to hear. You'll find sociable bridge just as addictive as the serious players find competitive bridge.

My motto is: "For a long and happy old age, it's better to have played bridge badly than never to have played at all."

From Hideko—I will be 70 this New Year's Day

I miss the girl I used to be so many years ago
With three inch heels and slim of build
And heart with laughter filled.

I love the woman I have become
With orthotic shoes and wide of build
And heart with loving filled.

And a good humored poem about this era in our lives:

At Seventy

At seventy backs ache, knees creak, minds wander and smiles broaden.
Parts that used to take care of themselves need tending.
And even though we don't want to believe it,
We are much further from the beginning than we are from the ending.

At seventy our children are grown up people
With jobs, lives, joys and troubles of their own.
Our grandchildren grow taller and smarter as we shrink and stretch.
And we all travel to places so far away
Our postcards take two weeks to deliver.
We smile as the kids tell us of their work, which we don't understand,
Of their friends, whose names we can't pronounce properly,
And of their aspirations which make us swell with pride and smile
     with memory.

At seventy we've grown up, but have not finished learning.
We seek simplicity and quiet joy
A walk through the park with a child in hand,
A stroll through a market in a foreign land,
Celebrations with family and friends,
A happy meeting of means and ends.
We pray for favorable test results, everyone's good health and a
     winning hand,
And just once in a while something going according to plan.
As we balance those we've lost with those we've gained.

At seventy, we forget where we put our keys,
Our cars and our appointment books.
But we know by heart how to fit the pieces of life together,
How to make lemonade out of lemons
And interesting patchwork patterns out of torn pieces of cloth.

At seventy our friends say we look "young and thin" before their
   cataract surgery
Our grandchildren tell us we are "old and round" before they learn to lie,
And we still seek engagement with a world that doesn't much care
   what we are doing.

At seventy we can enjoy a good book, if we can find our glasses;
A good meal with our friends, if we eat early enough;
A beautiful place with those we love, if we stay out of the sun;
And our own company.

At seventy precautions are second nature.
Social Security and Medicare are old friends.
What we want of ourselves and others seems possible,
And love, laughter and time are far more precious than jewels.

At seventy,
Injustice still rankles,
Empathy heightens,
Experience matters.
And loving kindness counts the most,
At seventy.
Caroline M. Simon, © September 2014

So you see, there are many ways to address the challenges of advancing age. Our blog offered a welcoming place that focused on the very issues women in their 70's are facing. With the urge to share, the time to organize their thoughts, and the anonymity the blog provided, women wrote their private thoughts in this public forum. They sought other points of view, needed support and, above all, social connection.

As we viewed these postings, we began to envision similar women in face-to-face encounters in a group setting. If we knew more about the women speaking, perhaps we could draw some conclusions relevant to the groups' demographics. Perhaps we could better describe this stage of life. We wondered how the conversation might change if the dynamics of the interactions were more spontaneous. Would similar topics be as salient? Would the immediacy of responses change the substance of the comments? To find out, we began our 70Candles conversation groups. We invite you to sit in with us in the chapter ahead.

CHAPTER TWO

70Candles Gatherings

My mission in life is not merely to survive,
but to thrive; and to do so with some passion,
some compassion, some humor, and some style.

Maya Angelou

After we reviewed the comments and posts on our 70Candles. com blog, we realized that our peers had much to share with each other. We wondered what would happen if we gathered together a dozen or so women our age to discuss in-person some of the topics that had surfaced on the blog. We knew we were a gutsy and voluble cohort—many of us had been proud participants in women's groups in the 1960's and 70's, and we were the first generation to enter the work force en masse. Maybe others would be as interested as we in discussing this new, uncharted decade. We gave it a go.

We solicited our friends for assistance and held our inaugural gathering in Philadelphia on April 2, 2011. So far, we have convened a total of 82 women in eight different groups, including several cities on the East Coast and in Texas. We sent an online invitation several weeks in advance of each scheduled date. You can read our invitation in Appendix A.

Trays of food and beverage choices were laid out before the group started. Participants were encouraged to come a little early to have time to meet each other, eat, and anonymously fill out index cards with some basic demographic information. They were asked to jot down answers to a set of questions about age, education, work, marital status, and current living situation. To learn more about what was on their minds, we offered the open-ended question, "What do you want to be sure we talk about today?" The question card is in Appendix B.

Once the women were seated in comfortable chairs arranged in a large circle we introduced ourselves, described our 70Candles project, and presented information about the recently described "longevity revolution." We pointed out that we women in our seventies are at the forefront of this new era, just ahead of the curve, and in so many ways we believe that we have a responsibility to pave the way for those who follow.

To begin the conversation, we asked each woman to share something significant about herself. After that, we had, in the back of our minds, five main questions and a final, summary query. As each session progressed, however, we willingly flowed with the conversational current as topics expanded and diverged. In no group did we actually get to all of these topics. Our questions were:

1. What was or is the meaning of work in your life? How does your idea of yourself (your identity) change when you cease to practice your profession/job?

2. How do you deal with/think about loss of function (memory, hearing, vision, balance, ability to multi-task etc.)?

3. How do you think others see you? How does it feel to be the oldest in the group?

4. What is life like for you today? What challenges? What joys? When do you feel at your best? What contributes to your well-being?

5. What advice would you have to give to younger women, perhaps to the baby boomers close on our heels, to prepare for turning 70? What do you know now that you wished

you'd known then? What do you wish you had done differently? Is there anything you wish you would have learned or accomplished that you can't do now?

6. Summary Question: What does it take to thrive in this, our eighth, decade?

PROFILE OF OUR GROUPS

Up to the time of this writing, we have conducted eight discussion groups, in five different cities: Philadelphia, New York City (2), Albany, New York (2), Ithaca, New York and Dallas Texas (2). A total of 82 women participated in these gatherings, ranging in age from 69 to 79, with an average age of 72.

You can see an age distribution graph in Appendix C.

Of the 82 women, racial distribution roughly mirrored national statistics. The majority, 66 (80%) were white, 8 (10%) were Black and 8 (10%) Latina. Each group was organized by a friend or an acquaintance, who in turn invited her own network of friends and acquaintances. Each group, then had its own largely homogeneous identity: one group was all African-American women; another consisted of Catholic women who identified as Mexican-American; another consisted of white women, many of whom attended the same New York City high school; another was all Jewish women who were members of the same congregation, etc. As you will see when we describe the conversations, there were certain advantages to this de facto homogeneity, as particular themes emerged from a few of the groups that were not reflected in others.

There was a range of educational accomplishment, but the preponderance of women, 62 of the 82 (75%) had completed higher education programs. In response to our question about schooling, we learned that 11 (13%) had graduated from high school, 6 (7%) had gone beyond high school to either junior college or vocational education, 25 (30%) had earned Bachelor's degrees, 25 (30%) had earned

Master's degrees, and 12 (15%) had some kind of professional degree, which included Ph.D.'s, and law degrees. One woman, in our "High School+" category described a degree earned in piano from a Russian conservatory, and the one woman in the category "Other" attended school until the ninth grade. A graph of educational achievement is in Appendix D.

Most of these women had been in the work force for many years. Some had worked "sporadically," but more than half (53%) had had careers that spanned an impressive 30-50 or more years. Another 13 (16%) had worked less than 30 years, while a quarter of the women provided no information in this regard.

About their current work life, 47 (57%) were retired. Nine (11%) checked two boxes indicating that they had retired from a career but were actively engaged in part-time work or significant volunteer pursuits. We call these "actively retired." Seventeen (21%) reported working part-time, while 9 (11%) continue working full time.

Combining the working groups, we see that 35 (43%) currently engage in some organized occupation. Most had had a career at one time, including teacher, attorney, professor, physician, nurse, business owner, pianist, and so on. You can see the distribution of career length on the graph in Appendix E.

SOME HIGHLIGHTS FROM THE GROUPS

WORK LIVES: Stories about jobs, careers, avocations, their evolution and denouement, were incredibly varied. There were nine women working full-time, several vowing never to retire. Many have found volunteer opportunities to use the skills they developed over the years. None of our sample now or ever identified themselves as "homemaker."

LIVING ARRANGEMENTS: These women lived mostly in houses (60%) in cities and suburbs (72%). Of the 77 women who responded to the question about their residences, 49 (60%) said they lived in a house, 3 (4%) in a town home, 13 (16%) in a condo, 12 (15%) in an apartment, and one in subsidized housing. Five did not respond to that item. Of the 65 responses received regarding location of their homes, 22 (34%) lived in urban areas, 37 (57%) in suburban areas, and 6 (9%) in rural locations.

While many women were still living in their original homes, some had already settled into new living arrangements, and others were in the process of doing so or were contemplating their options. No one was yet in some kind of assisted living arrangement. Where to live now and where to live next is a major issue for women in their 70's. This topic was discussed in the 70Candles.com blog, and as you will see in the next chapter, it was an important subject in our conversation groups.

CARING FOR SPOUSES: Of the 82 women, 47 (57%) were married, 20 (24%) had divorced, 11 (13%) were widowed, and 4 (5%) described themselves as single. All identified as heterosexual.

A remarkable number of women expressed concerns about their aging spouses. Some had nursed their husbands through years of debilitating illness and now, as widows, were reconstructing their lives. Others were standing by as their husbands' health declined, identifying each crisis as preparation for what might lay ahead. "God is preparing me," one said, giving her practice carrying out various household functions that had always been the province of her spouse, like seeing to auto repairs and managing household finances. She felt she was being given a chance to experience some of what it might be like to ultimately be on her own.

A few worried that the small signs they were detecting in their husbands' behavior seemed to augur mental decline, but there was no way to talk about that at home. They were anxious about the future. Others sought information about assistive devices for husbands with hearing loss. Other women, having lost a spouse after many years of being the primary caregiver, felt freed, finding new life rhythms among their women friends and pursuing travel adventures.

BE SURE TO TALK ABOUT THIS!

In response to the written, open-ended question, "What do want to be sure we talk about today?" the women offered a range of thoughts and queries that fell into a variety of topic areas. They were hoping for discussion about being this age, how to spend one's time, friendships and social networking, health issues, and loss. Here's how they broached these topics.

Being this age (15 comments)

> ...how people feel about being in their 70's. Life. Life and its alternatives.

> What do I want to do for the rest of my life? How to age gracefully. Aging gracefully...what is it...how to do it? How to live to be 80 & retire.

> Difficulty accepting not being a "young" person any more. How we redefine ourselves for the next phase in our life.

> What words describe us, as an alternative to "retirement." Coping with everyday problems. Transitioning into this stage of life. Accepting getting older.

> Our youthful future. How wonderful life is after 70. Life is terrific!

Occupation (9 comments)

> New outlets for women to get involved in. Volunteering. How to find a job.

> Focus for everyone on a particular activity or interest.

> Finding travel companions

> Life as caretaker of husband. Needing a purpose. Technology.

> Continuation of active, purposeful life—best path to take.

Friendships and Social Networking (9 comments)

Connections. How and where to find someone to date.

Keeping a community of friends for many years to come.

Being invisible...marginalized. Marginalization. Family interactions. Living the single life!

People who only talk about health issues.

Health (7 comments)

To fix, or not to fix. Facing mental and physical changes. Facing physical and mental changes.

Staying mentally and physically healthy. Why do we slow up physically, but not mentally? Sex.

Short term memory loss.

Loss (6 comments)

Loss. Dealing with friends who are failing. Loss of spouses and friends. How do we deal with illness and death grace-fully? Accepting loss and limitations. How to think positively about change and loss.

Finally, several worried and wanted to talk about how we handle crises and about "our fears."

Many left the question unanswered, but they wrote or told us in different ways that they just wanted to listen to what the group had to say.

THE CONVERSATIONS

We enlisted the aid of a scribe who took notes during each session, in an attempt to capture the essence of the discussion. The women were assured that any information we collected would be presented anonymously in any future writings, and they quickly accommodated to the presence of the note-taker (in each case a younger woman), who was free to participate in the discussion.

The groups were composed of mostly educated middle class women, most of whom had worked for many years. Although many seemed healthy and energetic, there were also recent widows still grieving, and there were several group members who were ill or recently out of the hospital themselves. They made the effort to attend because they wanted to take part in what they considered to be an important conversation.

The two-hour discussions gained momentum as participants responded to each question, and the women addressed each other as new ideas were voiced. There was laughter and good humored sharing, as well as sad and poignant moments. We all listened with interest and fascination as women described events in their lives, told where they'd come from, and what might be ahead. We heard anecdotes about families, jobs, friendships, marriages. There were concerns about living alone, possible future living arrangements, finances and grown children. The women spoke about facing aging and death, supporting sick and dying spouses, and losing friends and colleagues. These women were redefining their roles in their families and communities and were in various stages of constructing the path ahead.

In Chapter Three, we will describe the themes that emerged in more detail. Here, we'd like to share the feeling of being in such a gathering, for this was a unique experience for most. Rarely do women in their 70's have the opportunity to spend concentrated time with peers for the express purpose of discussing ourselves at this age.

One story triggered another, as the women, alert and engaged, responded and lent support to each other. They commiserated about loss of memory, everyone wary of incipient Alzheimer's, each thinking her memory issues must be worse than the others. They smiled as they reported what they had chosen to do with new found time…more hours to practice piano, a chance to actually be a "photographer" after a life-long hobby taking pictures, opportunities to travel where they'd always wanted to go, the pleasure of cleaning the house at leisure, starting to paint, to garden, and to be unrushed with grandchildren.

There were moments of sadness as people remarked about death and their struggles with the loss of dear friends and family members: lives changed completely when a spouse died; grief over a lost sister.

> *"My sister's passing recently has been a tumultuous experi-ence and it has made me value my remaining time here. Her death has sharpened that feeling for me."*

The group enjoyed the humor of exchanging ageist anecdotes. While some felt invisible in public settings, others had encounters that engendered attention. A cabaret actor stopped one woman who had been trying to keep her hair from appearing grey, to tell her he loved the way her locks matched her purple dress! Another woman felt flattered when a frequent delivery boy seemed to linger to talk with her...only to learn eventually, that she reminded him of his beloved great-aunt.

Lively banter ensued when we addressed the lessons we could offer the boomers and our children coming up behind us. One group said, "Phooey, let them work it out for themselves. This is for us!" Others had advice about coping in hard times that included medita-tion, yoga, painting, walks in nature, gardening, and sharing time with friends. Some were particularly distressed by illnesses, frailties, and loss of those they knew. Volunteering at the nursing home that one woman had been doing for many years became too difficult when resi-dents there were now people she knew well.

There were thoughts expressed about what might have been missed in life, like living on one's own for those who married right after college, or a real and cohesive career for those who completed high school and then had many jobs throughout their lives. The physi-cian who had devoted her life to her career regretted not having had time for friends all those years, but was happy to now be part of a welcoming book group of sorority sisters from her college days.

Women faced each day with very different attitudes. While one woman delighted in wearing sweats, not caring what people at the grocery store might think, another dressed meticulously, put on make-up and proudly walked out the door, *"feeling like an attractive woman."*

Women admitted how important their women friends were in their lives. One confided, *"I know I could survive without my husband, but I couldn't exist without my friends."* A recent widow invited her best friend to camp out at her home while her friend was transitioning from a house to an independent living setting. For the few months they were together the recent widow, who continued to work, loved coming home to a hot dinner; and her friend was delighted to have a home to keep organized, and a place to cook. They had a perfect reciprocal arrangement for a time.

The strength of old friendships was apparent. Women who grew up in the "Little Mexico" neighborhood in Dallas stayed connected to extended families through the years, long after they had moved to the suburbs. Other women returned to their home towns after college and shared life stages with old pals as their families grew. Now, in retirement, they continued their connections and met frequently for lunch and conversation. Many of the city women had moved from the suburbs and maintained alliances that had begun when their children were small. These women supported charitable causes together, took classes, participated in book clubs, and travelled in various groupings.

For readers who want to see a more complete description of the groups, we include a chart of demographic information in Appendix F.

This is not intended to be a scientific study. Our ideas and findings are not conclusive. In fact, there is an intentional integration of objectivity and subjectivity in our thoughts and our writing. Friends and acquaintances helped us set up the groups, arrange the time and place, and invite those they thought would enjoy participating in the group discussion. We did not hear from women seriously ill, clinically depressed, or with extremely negative outlooks. Our respondents were largely middle-class women. One hostess confided to us, *"There are some of our friends who are not as positive and not as healthy as we are—they didn't come today."*

The women who accepted our invitation to talk about this era of our lives came to our gatherings voluntarily, willing to share their critical life experiences with us and each other. As fellow travelers they were women open to new ideas, this kind of new experience, and honest, heartfelt sharing with us and each other.

They were us! The 70Candles groups echoed our own life stories and the opportunities we enjoyed, including the possibilities we and they envisioned for the eighth decade of life. We actually learned and grew and consolidated our own identities along with the members of our groups. Many suggested that groups like these should continue, even for men, as the beginning of a new format and way to process the on-going changes in our lives as we all grow older.

The gatherings were personal, emotional, and social in nature. Specifically, the women were largely accepting and non-judgmental. They were the experts, on their own lives, not us. The discussions used initial questions to start things off, but the results were free-ranging and spontaneous.

Our discussions and interactions with our two groups of women of color convince us, even further, that this 70Candles project must seek out and embrace more diversity in the future. There is much to learn in conversations with women of diverse ethnic, racial, and religious backgrounds. More integrated groups would yield rich conversation. We know we cannot generalize from this small sub-set of 82 women to all who enter their eighth decade, nor can we draw conclusions about any one woman.

The group discussion format is a useful tool to get us to the mirror, but far too slow and costly to be the only approach to the study of 70Candles women. We need larger groups, more diverse samples, improved methodologies, and a willingness on the part of researchers and policy makers to lay aside a priori assumptions about older women.

We must see things as they are. Our hope is that akin to individual or family case studies in psychiatry and psychology, we have generated some interesting, intriguing, and inspiring ideas and concepts which others can build upon and verify through wide-scale studies. We began with women in the U.S., but it is only a start. As we progress in our understanding of the 70Candles woman, we begin to wonder about the global woman—the women in China, India, Africa, and of all other nationalities, ethnicities, religions, and colors of the world. What are their lives like? What are their issues? How are they similar to and different from the women in the US with whom we have connected?

Those are questions for our next venture, for there is a different, indeed a higher, purpose to the work we present here. While we are learning about this decade of life for women, and describing it, we believe we are also enhancing it for ourselves and our participants, and now for you, our readers. We hope you can hear the laughter, see the tears as participants relate poignant experiences, realize their age-mates can relate, and have their own similar experiences and stories to tell. It is really fun, and powerful, to gather together. We women in our 70's, everywhere, have much to share!

70CANDLES WOMEN SPEAK

What an opportunity! Two hours, sitting in a circle with women, all of us the same age, all focused on the same topic—ourselves, in this era of our lives. So much laughter and joy in congregating like this, so evident in group after group. More spontaneous and nuanced than the blog entries, our conversations were living testimonials to the power that comes when 70 year-old women congregate in a loosely structured environment to share their lives. Responses before and after ranged from, *"creating a circle of women is critical,"* and *"...the support of friends is crucial,"* to *"I'm sometimes scared about being with people and talking about myself,"* and *"aging is easier when I know everyone else is going through what I am."* One woman summed up the experience when we asked her a year later what she remembered from the group she participated in. She said, *"I remember the cama-raderie, the sharing. By the end I was more relaxed and more self-accepting than I think I'd been in years. Thank you."*

Despite our individual differences, we were shaped by the same vibrant period of America's history, each of us born in the late 1930's and early to mid-1940's. "Their history was our current events," one participant said of her grandchildren. We've all been affected by whirlwind technological advances (and we mean television too, not only computers and smartphones), tragic wars, heartbreaking assas-sinations of national heroes, but most cogently, by second wave femi-nism that emerged when we were young adults. From the perspective of today, it's hard to imagine life before the birth control pill, safe and legal abortions, women physicians, lawyers, and professors, women T.V. anchors and heads of corporations, members of the U.S. Senate… but it's the world each of us knew well. The possibility of a female U.S. President was unthinkable!

While the overriding tone of the conversation groups was one of life-satisfaction and wide-ranging gratitude, eight distinct themes developed in each: (1) work and retirement; (2) ageism; (3) functional changes; (4) caretaking; (5) loss and the end of life; (6) future liv-ing arrangements; (7) social connections; and (8) grandparenting. We begin the remainder of this chapter by discussing each of these themes. We then move on to describe two special groups we conducted, one in Albany, New York for African-American women and one in Dal-las, Texas for American women of Mexican descent. You will see that the same themes emerged in each of the groups, across-the-board, but there were a few unique features definitely worth describing in the ethnically-specific groups. We end this chapter as we ended each con-versation group, asking participants what currently brings them the most joy in their lives, how they imagine or think about the future, and what advice they might have for those who follow in our footsteps. You will see that we rely extensively in this chapter on selected quotes from our participants, with limited commentary from us. It is our opinion that when the participants speak for themselves, the project we've been undertaking is at its most powerful.

WORK AND RETIREMENT

In each group we discussed our work lives and explored the ramifications of shifting direction with passing years. It is no accident that this is the longest section in this chapter. It is the issue that 70 year-old women in our groups talked about more than anything else. As the first generation of women in professions, we felt very different from our mothers. Most of our mothers did not work outside the home. Men counted on their wives to nurture and shepherd the children, cook meals, and keep their home running well. Husbands were the proud bread winners and considered it their duty to provide for the family. Women of our mothers' generation were not able to have their own bank accounts or check books. They couldn't independently buy a car or a house; they needed a man to stand behind such large purchases. In some cases, we learned from our participants, these issues have persisted even to recent times.

> *"I still couldn't buy a car under my name, in 2001, even though it was my own money. I went to the Title Company and paid to transfer the title to my name."*

> *"I had a full time job, but I never had credit cards until eight years ago."*

A wider range of career options opened up for us in the 1960's and early 1970's, when the feminist movement took center stage in America. Law schools, medical schools, business schools, and graduate schools in many fields all started admitting more women. Women ascended into the workplace from high school, from college, and from graduate schools.

As we entered the work world, we gradually broke down old

stereotypes and forged new identities—woman doctor, lawyer, psychologist, professor, banker, accountant, entrepreneur—even corporate executive. Women with and without college educations rose to positions of responsibility across the career spectrum. In our groups most of the participants had long and fulfilling careers, even as we raised our families.

It was interesting to consider how our identity had been affected by our life's work. Is our job who we are? Or is it a mutable facet of our being? The women in our gatherings shared disparate views and anecdotes on that subject.

> *"Work is not the paycheck or the W-2. Your profession is always with you…I have the worldview of a lawyer, even without the job title."*

As one woman was about to retire, after a long career as Dean of Students, a colleague said to her, "You won't know who you are when you wake up tomorrow." "He was wrong!" she proclaimed to us.

While the retired lawyer still views nuanced issues in the world through her analytic lens, the speech-language pathologist stays attuned to voices and speech patterns wherever she goes. The essence of each of us is embedded in a complex fabric that seems to extend beyond and outlast the office.

> *"As a scientific nutritionist, I am always practicing what I learned to do in college. It comes into play every day. I have to plan my husband's meals because he is diabetic. One of my children is dieting, so I have talked with her about how to do that. I haven't really left my career, even though I am not being paid."*

"I call myself a 'Social Worker without Borders,'" one woman declared as she described her role as the *"go-to"* person when her friends and neighbors face personal or medical crises.

Our participants demonstrated that there is a wide-spectrum of ways to approach the end of a career. One woman working full- time at a job she had had for years, when asked, declared to her boss that she would go out *"feet first."* By far the oldest person in that business, she felt fondness and respect from her colleagues. Another long-employed woman, a widow who still had to work as an office manager to support herself, was allowed flexibility so she could go home at lunchtime or alter the hours as she wished. One woman worked at the same fashionable department store from age 17, as a part-time trainee after school, until she was 71, finally parting when they offered her a generous retirement package. She had grown up in the accounting department, felt close to all her mentors there, and still felt occasional pangs of nostalgia when at home in her new role as caretaker of her husband. Some have moved from employment to family roles, helping with grandchildren who live nearby.

Half of our participants have stayed committed to their jobs, working part-time or full-time still:

> *"I am working as hard as I ever had. I have a big fear of moving on to the next phase of my life and retiring."*

Another says she is not afraid to retire:

> *"I just don't want to. I love what I do."*

Others adopt a gradual approach:

> *"As I tiptoe toward retirement, I have been slowly cutting back on my hours and responsibilities…but I'm still not ready to end it all. Gradual seems best. I need to have a better view of what might lie ahead."*

Some felt ambivalence and considerable angst about leaving their work lives:

> *"I don't make transitions easily…As soon as I stopped working, I immediately wanted to go back; I missed my friends, I wasn't sure I liked retirement. Then, my replacement went on leave and I was asked to come back. It only took 5 minutes and I wanted out. "*

> *"Teaching was my whole being. What do I want to do next?"*

Others described a struggle with the change:

"When I retired at 71, it was a very hard adjustment. I missed friends. It was very hard to let go."

A few were asked to leave, or were offered irresistible buyouts:

"After the downturn in 2008 they wanted us older folks to take a buyout, which I took, but that has been a transition."

Several had a change of heart:

"I taught elementary school for 32 years, retired, and after five years got so bored that I went back to work teaching college students. I love it."

"...joyous at first, I was looking forward to more adventure. I had great times; Grandparenting, traveling, and exercising were kind of it. Now I need to do something more."

A number left their jobs with certainty or with goals for the future:

"I retired early and I knew wanted to learn to paint. I went to the senior center for lessons. It is a passion, and I've stuck with it."

"...I received a call from a favorite client who wanted to have a meeting so I could present my findings and recommendations. I said, calmly but firmly, 'I have another commitment at that hour.' I suddenly realized that my yoga class was more important than this wonderful client."

And many felt a huge relief:

"Oh no, I don't feel guilty."

"Being Executive Director of a non-profit...was a weight on my shoulders. How good it felt after I retired; it's a gift."

"Before there was so much to worry about, and now...it's true what they say...I can take a minute and stop and smell a rose if I want to."

"I don't see retirement as an ending, but rather as an expanding...Now I think it's more like putting new tires on a car, re-tiring, liberating!"

Many have found satisfaction in volunteering: reading or tutoring in schools, serving as docents at art museums or children's museums, engaging in political action, participating in charitable organizations, or helping others in informal ways. Inconveniences were noted, as well as satisfaction, like the long hilly climb from the museum parking lot to the front door, and the mixed attitudes of docents at a new museum who, after extended training, were disappointed that they were not to play as important a role as they had expected. But these endeavors provided purpose, new learning, and social engagement valued by the women in this stage of their lives.

In spite of any resistance on our part, digital technology and the cyber-world have blown through society and carried us alongside. We aren't "computer natives" like the toddlers of today, or "computer immigrants" like our grown children, but some call us "computer refugees." We have certainly crossed over into contemporary culture, and as many of our participants noted, all our future options are colored by that fact.

One woman opined, *"When you quit work you need to retire to something."* Another responded, *"There are many places where you are needed and can make a difference."*

As we shift from our previous work lives to the decades beyond, there are countless ways to find redefinition. Our women had thoughtful ideas on the subject. They acknowledged the strengths that we bring with us and the variety of ways we can apply our accumulated wisdom and experience.

"It's OK to have a 70 year old mind—we're wise and experienced."

"I feel more capable and effective now."

"Keep learning, because that will keep you young."

"I worried about how I could continue to use my brain, but it turns out opportunities abound."

What shall we do when we no longer pursue our careers? We might retool, retrain, pursue new ventures, or volunteer where there's a need. *"Optimism matters. Know that there are possibilities ahead,"* said one woman. Other comments:

"I'm into new adventures. I have found that life is very exciting now, and I'm doing things I never imagined I would do."

"I like the idea of mentoring others as my next stage."

"I am a photographer," a former attorney confessed, beginning a whole new chapter in her life.

"With age has come experience and wisdom to pass along to younger people. By being a good listener, you can be a catalyst to help them sort things out. They know the answers; they just need help finding them. We have inspirational status."

"Connect, connect, connect with family, friends, and especially women friends. Relate to people of all ages. Have several different communities."

"Make younger friends. Interact with different kinds of people. Don't marginalize anyone."

"There is something good in every day; find it, notice it, wonder at it, give it, be it."

"Accept your friends with all their frailties as they age. Don't focus on what was or what might be."

"Bring energy to whatever you do—it keeps you going."

"I haven't figured out how to give back, to give to society now that I'm no longer working. I know I'll figure it out eventually."

"I think an issue for women our age is the discrepancy in work trajectories between us and our husbands—it's problematic when one's ready to retire, and the other isn't."

"I retired from New York State seven years ago. I had a long list of things to do when I retired, like cleaning out the closet. The list keeps growing, but I never get to any of it. I'm just as busy now as I was then."

"Where's my identity? It's about having the courage to change careers, to grow, to create new options. That's what's different about our generation. A generation ago, those who worked stayed with what they did. Our generation evolves. We had the freedom to change and the options available are much broader."

AGEISM

Anecdotes about ageism brought forth laughter and mutual acknowledgement from the women in our groups. The term "Ageism" was first identified and defined by Robert Butler in 1969 as "Prejudice and discrimination toward elderly people." Examples abound to this day. We hold ageist views about ourselves and others. Why do we view older people as less competent, weaker, more needy? Perhaps our society focuses so much on external signs of physical strength and youthful appearance that it doesn't appreciate the value of internal virtues. So often comments we hear and actions perpetrated upon the elderly don't match our own perception of ourselves. Here we are, more knowledgeable than ever before in our lives, with the benefit of a long perspective, and with so much to contribute. And still, ageism stares us in the face.

"At my institution, there's an unstated policy that anyone over 55 won't get a job. We're thought to be out of touch with the younger population and assumed to be lacking in the necessary technical skills."

A management consultant wondered, *"If clients knew I was 70, would they still hire me?"*

One woman wanted a job, but her hair was gray. She thought that dying her hair would make her more desirable. And she might be right.

The 71 year old full time attorney said, *"People might not listen to me if they knew I was 71, so I keep it to myself."*

"It's hard to be in the business world at 70—it's just not that accepting."

It is clear that social change is needed to educate about and eliminate ageism, particularly as the population ages and the baby-boomers reach their senior years. The place to start is with us—sharing our stories and raising awareness first among ourselves and then among others.

FUNCTIONAL CHANGES

Good health affects our image of being old, so we have an advantage over previous generations. Our generation of women is in better health, in general, than our foremothers. We've had the benefit of advances in sanitation and in medicine in the last century, and we pay attention to recommendations about nutrition. We've benefitted from fluoride in our water and lifelong dental care, allowing us to still have our teeth. And we exercise. Our physicians know more about normal changes in the aging process, and they stand ready to intervene if needed.

First we notice our grown kids seem taller...or more likely, we are shrinking a bit, to the delight of our grandkids who stretch to see us eye-to-eye.

What about changes in our stamina? Those dates with young grandchildren, an unmatched joy, can really wear us out. A nap can sound like a very good idea.

Our physical selves typically feel the passage of time. Women shared their observations about changes they experience. Losing balance? Less steady? Sensible shoes are a must. Some of us now need to hold the banister when walking down stairs and notice they now take care when stepping off curbs. Gotta love those ramps! And it doesn't help to have bi-focal or progressive lenses that alter space perception with the tilt of a head.

Whadja say?? Hearing loss creeps up quietly, usually gradually. Cope by letting others know. Admit it to others, and explain how they can help.

Notice that you need more light to read? Eyeglasses? Contact lenses? Cataracts? Macular changes? What a challenge it is to drive at night with those Van Gogh-brilliant halos around every light source. Whom can you count on for night driving? Not noticing small bits of dirt on pots or smudges on mirrors anymore? At the very least, everyone in our groups needed reading glasses. Some found large print books were a treat, as are the font options on all our electronic readers. For serious macular degeneration there are magnifying cameras that light the way.

Women mentioned medications, flat-heeled shoes, losing height, and incontinence.

> *"I lose my balance now and can no longer multi-task. I can't seem to talk on the phone and follow a recipe at the same time, for example. I need to hold on to the banister when I'm on the stairs. But really, I accept these limitations."*

> *"I am a long-distance race-walker, and it's hard to walk for seven hours without peeing. I don't drink enough fluids, which is bad; I also take a pill, some kind of herb, starting about two weeks before a race." [Everyone wanted to know the name of the pill, but the woman couldn't remember!]*

> *"I can't get down on my knees and get up very easily."*

> *"I don't have as much strength—something that is heavy now for me isn't heavy for my kids."*

> *"I don't want to climb things anymore. I'm afraid to fall."*

And do we forget things?

"Once the list gets to the third item, it's best to write things down...and keep that piece of paper in sight, before it too fades into the black hole of...lost socks."

We all have trouble remembering as we used to. In fact most everyone chimed in on the topic of memory loss, with much glee in laughing together about our foibles in this regard. Funny stories abounded. Every woman was sure at one time or another that dementia was just around the corner or had already arrived. At each group we asked, "How many of you think your memory loss is worse than everyone else's?" Every hand went up in every single group. Surprising perhaps to younger people, but not to us, was the good humor with which these topics were discussed. Sharing brings relief and a tremendous feeling of sisterhood.

Then there's the difficulty of locating items that aren't immediately visible. Where were they placed/misplaced? Where did someone else stash them?

"Just today I was sure that someone had stolen my purse, especially because I wasn't sure whether or not I'd locked my front door when I left the house."

"So many indoor mysteries. Why did I come into this room?"

"Ah, the agony and the ecstasy: The feeling of euphoria when what was lost is found or remembered."

"It's never too late to learn new things. The challenge is to remember them."

Participants offered strategies that help:

"My advice to others is have a sense of humor, and, above all, don't panic."

"Admit, own up, acknowledge, do the best you can with it."

"I try to never bemoan what I can't do."

"I cope by letting people know. A speech therapist with a hearing loss, oh boy."

"I have to carry around a tablet because I have to write everything down."

"I carry a calendar everywhere."

"I put all birthdays on my phone. Then I set the phone for reminders, so I can send out a text right away."

"Kindles and Nooks can be helpful for altering font style and size."

"I use Post-it notes."

"When I can't remember something, I use the 1,2,3, system: (1) It will come into my head if I wait long enough. (2) I could recognize it on a multiple choice test, but may not get it on my own—give me a few minutes to try. (3) No way, I'm not even going to try."

"Stop me if you remember that I told you this before."

CARETAKING AND THE CLUB SANDWICH GENERATION

As longevity has increased, many of us find ourselves still having our parents in our lives. As they age we become their caregivers, even as we continue to emotionally support and nurture our children, our grandchildren, and often our spouses, as well. This can be a continued joy, or an emotionally taxing responsibility, especially if there is slow deterioration of mind and body in the more elderly. Most of our parents did not have that experience with our grandparents.

We hear how some women shift all their attention to the care of elderly parents. Some cease working and take on the task, single-handed. Others accept support from siblings or community services. Our participants talked of life-as-usual put on hold when this duty calls. And participants spoke of confronting dying and death and their inevitable impact.

Of the women in our groups who were worried about the health of their partners or spouses, many were actually nursing husbands who were quite ill.

"For those of us with spouses, we're at the stage of facing unknowns. Today is wonderful, but what's tomorrow going to be? There are signs you might see that the other person doesn't want to acknowledge. There's a sense of denial about things that are happening."

"My parents lived in Chicago; when Mom went through five years of poor health I shuttled between Chicago and here. I did the same thing for my Aunt for a year and a half. This is the first year in nearly a decade that I'm free of caretaking. There are no more elderly people that I will need to take care of."

"I was widowed—after 37 years together—he was my partner in every sense of the word. We did everything together. He became very sick in his last years of life. It was a long and arduous decline—I took care of him, my parents, and a sibling. You do what's in front of you in life. You need to wake up happy—pretty miserable not to."

"I was widowed. I had a great husband; I was his caretaker, and I also took care of his sister:"

"I have a husband who needs some pampering; he has some health issues. These responsibilities fall upon the wife."

"The struggle is that I have to be away from the home to keep my job, but I can't leave my husband."

"It's God's way of preparing us. You learn to be patient with a sick person, learn to slow down for him. I have to take care of him, and that's a fact."

"My husband did everything—now that he's sick, I have to learn to get around everywhere. I have to do everything."

"When Mom started getting sick, my husband cooked dinner and helped at home. My husband helped me with my mother until the day she died."

"At 71, I'm taking care of my mother-in-law. I never thought I would be that person."

LOSS AND THE END OF LIFE

No one in our groups was a stranger to illness or death. In fact, there were women among our participants who had recently been in the hospital, others were cancer survivors. Some were still grieving recent losses. The conversations about loss were brief, but sobering.

"Be an advocate for yourself. Don't be defeated by any disability."

"I had surgery on Monday, and I am so out of it still. But I have been so aware of my vulnerability lately, because I really value my activity."

"When we, or those around us, become ill we feel loss of control. Just know you can't control the illness or the health-care system. Yes, it can be sad."

"The biggest thing is our health—osteoporosis and Alzheimer's are two big concerns."

"It's so hard to see people losing their faculties—people with Alzheimer's. It's excruciating to watch this."

"Loss is something we all need to deal with."

"At the loss of a partner or dear friend it helps to turn to your friends for support."

"Death...I really haven't come to grips with this. It's happening to so many people our age. How do we have the strength to deal with it? How can I be strong for everyone and push aside my own feelings to be there for others? Sometimes I can do it, sometimes I can't sleep...I want to find the strength."

"This has been a couple years with close people in my family dying—my sister, my brother-in-law. Very difficult. It affects everything in my life. It's a whole different thing than losing a parent. I still think about them. I'm left with such sadness and vulnerability. Those people can't be replaced."

"Over the past few years, I have had four close friends die, and it is really hard. And because of our age it's going to happen more often."

"When my partner was dying—7 or 8 years ago—I really started thinking about death."

"Death—You have to do a lot of talking to yourself to get through it—it takes a long time."

"Sometimes you never get over grieving. Little reminders always come up."

"Each year, there are close friends that die. There is a bit of a shadow that we can't get away from, of death."

"People are dying. I find this difficult; this loss is permanent, it's not so easy to get the strength."

"Death is the next really big thing that is going to happen in my life."

LIVING ARRANGEMENTS

Downsizing comes in many forms. Once children have left home, many feel they need less space, fewer rooms to take care of. They imagine something smaller and easier to manage. Moving from the large family home, at last, to a smaller cottage? A cozy apartment? No longer enjoy those flights of stairs, or need those extra bedrooms? The women in our groups described the choices they were making, and we further explore the wide range of living options available in Chapter Five ahead.

For those down-sizing, there is always the issue of disposing of a lifetime of collections. The sorting through becomes a veritable trip down memory lane, sometimes joyful, sometimes not.

"We are downsizing," announced one woman. Others could relate:

"I don't want to leave this mess for others to deal with. I'm starting the shedding."

The process of discarding can be very emotional, but when it becomes clear that one's children really don't want all that's been saved for them over the years, the "stuff" must go. Giving things away, holding yard sales, donating to charities, or just putting things out on the curb for treasure scavengers—it helps to imagine all those discarded items passing forward into the lives of others. In fact, very little is ever actually missed. A friend was asked what had happened to the decades of treasured family photos that had lined both sides of a long hallway in their home. Surely, there was no room for them in their lovely new one-bedroom independent living community. She said, *"Oh, our son just scanned them all and put them in a digital photo frame that sits on our living room table."* Modern technology, hooray!

Choices about where to live next depend on a number of variables:
- *whether a woman is alone, or with a partner*
- *financial means*
- *location—near family members, or friends, or among other retirees*
- *urban, suburban, or rural*
- *how compact and efficient*
- *physical space and layout: one floor rather than 2-story*
- *need for accessibility and incorporation of universal design*
- *access to transportation*

Where might we live in the future? Participants agreed that this issue first came into focus when they neared 70 and faced the reality of old age. For many, it is a source of significant anxiety.

Two women, in different cities, proclaimed that they were incredibly happy living on their own. One was an artist who was single, and the other a woman recently divorced after a difficult marriage. *"Alone at last,"* she declared.

One woman, still employed, moved into the house with her daughter and teen-age grandson. She felt independent but still tied down as she transported her grandson to his various activities while her daughter worked. Another very creative woman sold her home and moved into the downstairs apartment of her daughter and family. She enjoyed the proximity and interactions with her two grandsons as well as various academic pursuits during the winter months, but she got away from late spring to early fall to a small cabin she purchased upstate.

Many had doubts and questions about what would be best for them.

> *"I don't have children. My home is here; my friends are here. Should I go back to the city where my siblings are? Do I go back...and when? I own a home. Do I want to move into something else, and if so, here or elsewhere?"*

> *"I live by myself in an apartment with steps and I think, 'Am I going to have to move from this beautiful apartment because I can't get into it anymore?'"*

Some offered advice:

> *"Be knowledgeable about your family and personal financial information. Our kids are nervous about taking care of us. We need to plan for long-term care, care at home, and living accommodation options."*

Several were experimenting, and working out the best decision over time:

> *"My husband and I moved to Florida when we both retired, but we came back to be closer to children. Going to Florida for early bird specials was not my idea of fun. We're happy to be back home and now plan to stay put."*

One woman lived in the town in which she was born; all her children and grandchildren were there; and that is where she knew she and her husband would live out their lives. But where to go when children are spread around the country? The women in our groups continue to grapple with this dilemma:

> *"My son and his family are in Wisconsin; my daughter is in West Virginia. I moved here on my own for a job. This isn't home to my kids. They both have families; as I get older the biggest issue is where do I live? And when do I make the shift?"*

> *"I don't want to leave my friends. My children can come see me."*

> *"I don't want to make my kids feel obligated if I moved closer to them."*

> *"Kids don't live in any place for very long, anyway, so what's the point of moving to be near to them?"*

> *"I sold the family house two years ago and now I live in a two family house with my daughter and her husband and the two boys who are the light of my life. It's well worth it."*

> *"I thought about moving, but then I realized that this is home, this town has adopted me. At this point of my life, uprooting is very challenging…the older you get…very traumatic."*

Many prefer a choice that will allow continued "aging in place." They'd like to feel a sense of community and have convenient access to shops and services. And, very importantly, they'd like to know there is transportation they can count on when they no longer transport themselves.

> *"My fear is not being able to drive…I want to be able to get around. Nothing is more scary than that. And I don't even like to drive!"*

We had predicted most of the themes in advance of our groups, but not this one. Housing arrangements were just not something that had occurred to us, perhaps because of our own current, stable living situations. But our eyes were opened. Relocation or its prospect is an issue for 70 year-old women.

SOCIAL CONNECTIONS

By far the most powerful message imparted in our groups was the importance of other women in the lives of our participants.

As our conversations gathered momentum, even those new to the assembled crowd began to connect. Ideas and themes pivoted from one person to the next. Women responded with warmth and empathy as they recognized similarities or contrasting issues in their own lives. They offered advice to each other and thought about their own impact on generations ahead. They emphasized the strength they received through their ties to other women.

These women, who statistically should expect to outlive their male partners, knew that other women were their life-line. They valued and declared great trust in their women friends.

> *"Maintaining relationships with women has been really important for me. They have been the core of my life."*

> *"Women need women. Communicating with women is healthy."*

> *"Men don't have friends the way that women do. The strength of womanhood—reaching out to, getting advice from, each other—makes us as vital as we are."*

> *"Sustaining emotional connections. These are crucial factors."*

> *"Keep meeting new people all the time, even if they turn out to be acquaintances and not best friends."*

> *"I have a great group of single women—divorced or otherwise—and we've done a lot of stuff together."*

"Isolation is horrible; socialization is so important."

"Isolation is bad. I never want to be in the house. I want out be out with my friends."

The importance of social connections, friendships with women our age, was the single topic about which there was absolute agreement throughout our conversation groups.

GRANDPARENTING

Grandparenting is a particular form of social connecting, with wide variation among our participants, although all were grandmothers or "aunties." While serious illness and caring for the elderly can confront us with our own mortality, the wondrous contrast of time with grandchildren—time that can evoke the child within us—was mentioned repeatedly by many (but not all). Those for whom grandparenting is a key part of their lives now discussed the joy that comes from reading favorite children's books once again, reminiscing about our own childhoods, giving rapt attention *to "the smallest sea shells and pebbles and the grandest rainbows and clouds."* Caring for and enhancing the well-being of young people is one example of the "generativity" described by developmental psychologist, Erik Erikson. Many developmental theorists concur that such activities are mutually beneficial.

Our women described and embodied three kinds of grandmothers: (1) Those who live for their grandchildren; (2) those who love their grandchildren, but do not consider them to be the end-all or be-all of their lives; and (3) those who don't want to babysit or really be too involved. Here are some comments that exemplify each of these "grandma types."

"We have moved to live near our children and grandchildren. It has been a very positive experience. Our grandchildren have gotten to know us, and we have been able to play a

role in their childhoods. We delight in teaching them what we can, and we are able to do special things with each of them. We hope these adventures will be remembered in the family archives."

"I love being with my grandchildren more than I loved being with my own children."

"My granddaughter is my life."

"My grandson makes me smile. We Skype. He is three and can finally converse."

"I miss the grandchildren terribly."

"To live near my grandchildren I would have to split myself in two because my children live in different places."

"Living demographics make it difficult for us to maintain our relationships with our children and grandchildren. I feel like my children don't know me anymore, and also, I feel like I don't know them anymore. I go to buy my daughter or grand-daughter a birthday present and I don't know what to get because I don't know what their interests are."

"I'm worried that our grandkids have too many distractions and are losing traditional values; they're not attending church, and there's nothing I can do about it."

"I'm proud that my grandkids have made an effort to learn our language."

"The younger generation doesn't realize what we went through to get where we are now."

"I love my grandchildren, but I do not want to babysit. There's a reason I sent my children to daycare."

AFRICAN AMERICAN WOMEN

Well into this project, a younger African-American friend admonished us that our participants to-date had been all white women. Yes, we noticed that. But her comment crystallized for us not only that we wanted, of course, to hear from women of color, but also that there was power that came from homogenous groups, at least for this age cohort. When ten or twelve graduates of the same high school congregated, for example (in this case an almost exclusively white high school in those days), when members of the same synagogue assembled, there was an instant "relaxed energy" that we wish we could reproduce for you on these pages. It was palpable. It was joyous. There was an immediate sense of relief—aha, now we can talk about what matters with women just like me! In truth, this homogeneity happened accidentally. We would ask someone to organize a gathering, and then that person would invite group members of her choice. This is the nature of a "convenience sample." But we think in the end, and into the future, this is a hallmark of our project. And, perhaps with equal importance, we can then look across groups and identify patterns and themes that may approach universality—although we realize we are not conducting empirical research. So what happens when 70 year-old women of non-white ethnicities gather together? What is the same and what is different? Our sample is small but extremely powerful. We look forward to gathering together many more such groups.

Our first was assembled by a friend of the admonishing friend in upstate New York. Like our other groups, the participants would be described demographically as middle class women in their 70's. In this case, they were African-American women born and raised during the Jim Crow racial segregation era in various parts of the U.S. They also resided in an area with many low-income Blacks, but with a small percentage like themselves, well-educated, professional women. At first (although we all laughed when we noted they were better dressers than anyone who had attended our other groups), the issues were exactly the same. The energy was equally high, the atmosphere joyful, the themes that emerged profoundly similar.

Several were taking care of very sick relatives:

*"...with my husband having brain and back injuries, and a
97 year old aunt, I have struggled with how to make deci-*

sions when you love more than one. There are some certain hard decisions that you have to make ... "

"My husband, who is a bit older, has developed Alzheimer's. I need to find purpose in my life, broader than staying at home as a caretaker. A job, maybe? I would love to have some advice on how to find purpose in my life."

There was gratitude for the support of friends:

"Life is good for me. I live alone, but I have friends."

"...I had to go to the hospital....I was about to leave my house, my phone rang. My friend called and was surprised that I was driving myself. She said, 'Wait 20 minutes, and I will come get you.' She took me to the hospital and called all the key people in my life. It is good sometimes to surround yourself with people who love you, not just know you, but also care about you."

One woman noted that *"many women of color wind up living alone as they age and may need help staying connected with others."*

Much attention was focused on where participants lived now and what they saw and hoped for as next steps. Like participants in our other groups, one woman acknowledged, *"I realize that wherever I go next, is where I'll go last."* Different from our other groups was the element of race when it came to their current place of residence. Keep in mind that this was upstate New York, not New York City,

"I live in Saratoga, so I'm not blessed with having Black friends."

[This city] *"is more diverse now, but back when I first moved here, you couldn't live in some regions, and you could only work in three schools in the area."*

"You have to learn to live in a community that is not diverse, and become a part of the (White) whole, without isolating yourself from the Black community."

"I would like to be in a place where we are not so ill represented."

"I have become accustomed to not seeing anyone who looks like me, but it still bothers me."

They felt that there "should be more discussion about segregation in this part of the country." And they recommended that our conversation groups, in the future, be more integrated. They gave examples of "sub-conscious white privilege" that is ignored and the subtle racism they still experience.

"Race issues transcend ageism for us. Until that understanding is basic, we can't move forward."

"I'm not sure if White people 'get it.' The experience of being Black in this social system is a very emotional one."

Some felt that *"age may be the last 'ism' to be recognized by society-at-large."* But, at the same time, all agreed that *"Racism supersedes ageism for us."*

Finally, in the way of summary, they said jovially, *"Age is a number and an attitude."* And, *"it was great to meet new people and hear other people's points of view."* In perhaps a more reflective and urgent vein, they concluded by agreeing that it is the obligation of 70 year-old women of color to pass on their personal histories to the next generations—not to perpetuate a sense of victimhood, but rather to celebrate the opportunities they've had and how far they've come. They expressed both anger and perplexity at younger African-Americans *"who choose not to take advantage of the opportunities they now have."* Their advice to their grandchildren is *"Get an education!! Everything else will come!"*

These 70-year old Black women and their age-mates were teenagers when Rosa Parks refused to move to the back of the bus and Brown vs. the Board of Education was litigated. Many would say they embody the American Dream; all would understand they have stories to tell.

WOMEN OF MEXICAN DESCENT

We sat around a large square table at the Cathedral de Guadalupe in downtown Dallas. Jane and Ellen, with eight women, all of whom preferred to be referred to as *"Americans of Mexican descent."* The mood relaxed as soon as we closed the doors to the maelstrom of Sunday worshipping families travelling through the halls of the Cathedral.

All of the participants were born in Mexico and arrived in the U.S. as youngsters. Several knew each other from childhood days in the "Little Mexico" neighborhood of Dallas. These women had been encouraged by their parents to complete their Catholic high school education so they could get a good job. And work they did, for many years. Each at our table, like the other women in our conversation groups, identified as middle-class and educated. Most had former long standing careers from which they were now retired.

The majority of topics that emerged throughout our discussion were familiar to us from our previous groups, but some themes were unique. In particular, the women spoke of their very strong cultural identity. They had warm, nostalgic feelings for the Mexican communities of their youth, where *"we didn't know we were poor." "What is poor?"* one asked. She had a new dress at Christmas, at Easter, and for her birthday, and she got new shoes twice a year. Her home was comfortable, she was well fed, and her family taught her strong values. The children felt extremely safe and secure in their Mexican neighborhood. Doors were left unlocked, and keys were left in the car *"in case someone needed to borrow it."* They noted that *"people have more 'things' now, but those things own us,"* for *"now we need gates and locks."*

Families watched out for all the children and for each other, across generations. And caretaking continued today to be an important theme for this group of participants. Many had or were caring for elderly mothers, and several were nursing their sick husbands. Some had stopped work they enjoyed in order to take on these responsibilities. They noted that some of their brothers and spouses had served in Viet Nam, were exposed to Agent Orange there, and had long suffered various lung and heart problems. They mentioned spouses, siblings, and close family friends who helped shoulder some of the caretaking burden. One woman said, with heads nodding around the table, *"We may be the last generation devoted to our parents. Our kids will probably put us in nursing homes."*

The women described proudly the strength of the Mama in the homes they grew up in. When older children went to work, they would bring home their paychecks and, along with their father, hand the money over to their mother who would then give each an allowance and take care of all the bills.

The women in our group, like their mothers, aspired to be *"muy mujeres"*—a kind of super woman. They prided themselves, and were admired by others, for taking good care of their husbands and children, cooking well, especially making great tortillas, keeping a spotless home, and even capably wielding a hammer! And remember, these were also women with careers.

Above all, faith had always played a major role in their lives. As they spoke of God watching over them and taking care of them, they described the gratitude, optimism, and hopefulness that were built into the fabric of their religious convictions and therefore their lives. These were women with very positive spirits, thankful that they had led *"good lives."*

Many worried that their children and grandchildren had lost touch with the church and with the values instilled there. They described inter-marriages and less time for church activities in this busy era, when kids and families were involved with sports and distracted by technology and social media. They nostalgically recalled naming their own daughters Camilla and Isabella and Sophia, and now their granddaughters are named Ashley and Caitlin and Madison.

We left inspired by these energetic women—their long marriages, longer work histories, and their pride and sincere love for their roots and their progeny.

JOY AND SADNESS

First Joy. We asked every woman, in each of the groups, to share with us what brings her the most joy now and what makes her most grateful. Grandparenting is a deep joy for many 70 year-old women. Long term marriages tend to be better than ever. Women-bonding, extended family connections, and for some, faith communities, provide deep satisfaction. And then there are the idiosyncratic hot tips for enhancing well-being, such as the women who tells herself *"NEXT!"* when something goes awry and she wants to move on. We hope the following quotes will give you a better sense of the range of responses than any commentary we could possibly make.

> *"My granddaughter. I'm so happy with all she's accomplished and so proud of how good and kind she is. I must say I have more fun with my granddaughter than I had with my daughter."*

> *"My family. I feel so fortunate that both children and their families live in this city."*

> *"For me it's playing tennis and being in a book group."*

> *"In a global sense, I feel I have a positive impact through my work. I also find great joy from concerts, plays, and movies."*

> *"There's no one answer for me. Grandchildren; friends; doing good work that makes a difference; going to a great play or concert; singing..."*

> *"Life! You wake up every day. Look where we live—it's incredible."*

> *"Consciously I'm just generally grateful for the life I have. It's great to remember that every day. It's been worse. It wouldn't be great without the worse."*

> *"I'm grateful for science and what my cochlear implants have done for me, as compared to what I would be without them."*

"Some days I have a hard time dealing with another wrinkle or physical limitation, but each night I list ten things I'm thankful for from that day. It could be as basic as my arms and legs working, or the weather was beautiful."

"My children bring me joy, so much brings me joy. I feel lucky to be healthy and have good friends."

"Friends who accept me for who I am."

"A husband I've been with for well over half of my life, and we still laugh together every day."

"Joy comes from knowing that I have accomplished something that day—learned, shared, seen—the little things."

"We can all be grateful for something. Like, my digestion is working; the system has its own serotonin. Thank you, liver. My tendonitis is bad, but the other tendons are doing well."

"I am so fortunate to have been born to my parents."

"I feel grateful, blessed, lucky; I love living. Every day is a joy."

"My life is so rich now."

"I have a wonderful husband and family, and I will never be bored. I love to walk, to meditate. I'm grateful I can be grateful."

"My husband has been an advocate for me."

"My friends. Somebody calls or comes by almost every day."

"I feel joy from the outdoors. If I can't go out or see outside, I'm depressed."

"I'm grateful to be blessed with a really good sense of humor. My family has this sense of humor; it's so great."

"When things are low it's the drive to be creative that keeps me going."

And There is Also Sadness. No one can expect to avoid difficult passages in life. In response to our request for personal examples of joy and gratitude, one or two women would invariably remind the group that life is not always a bed of roses. Therefore, we include in this section some of the disappointments and regrets that were expressed as women movingly shared sadness and fears. Not unexpectedly, the greatest fears tended to be about losing loved ones and being alone.

> *"We have a group of friends, and we recently got together to celebrate a birthday. As I looked around the room, I realized everyone has been like a brother or sister to me for the last 40 years. I couldn't bear the thought of them not being there for me. And I thought 'I hope I go first.'"*

> *"If were by myself, if I had to run my life alone, I'd be nervous."*

> *"I'm divorced, but 25 years ago I met an amazing man who is 81 years old, but acts like he's 20. I'm nervous about what my life will be like without him."*

> *"Recently, I dread being alone."*

> *"I hate being alone. It's a couple's world."*

> *"If you've been alone and want to try to meet someone at our age, it's hard."*

Many were worried about health issues, especially about losing mental capacity.

Some resented seeming "invisible" to others.

> *"That's what makes people old—when they don't have anything to do...no place to go, nothing to read. Nobody needs you. When you become irrelevant, invisible."*

> *"The thing that does bother me a little is that I feel like a non-person. I mean, I don't like it when I go into a place and no one flirts with me anymore. It's fun to have someone flirt with you!"*

THE FUTURE

Our women, each and every one, envisioned more ahead. They were not always clear about what the future might hold, but they seemed optimistic and empowered to try new things and explore new places. That optimism was frequently tinged with sadness, as 70 year-old women dealt with the loss or decline of family members and friends at an accelerated pace. The more sanguine were able to face death and illness head-on and acknowledge it as a part of life.

"I know I'm more capable and effective now than I've ever been."

"I have come to the full recognition that I now have choices and opportunities that I didn't have before."

"It's about changing the purpose. Instead of ascending the mountain, I now feel fine about traversing the top of the mountain."

"I think age is a state of mind. I want to live like my mother and wear high heels until I'm 88."

"It's important to have vital youthful friends, although it's harder for us to meet younger people and establish relation-ships. This is a goal."

"I would like to be as independent, capable, opinionated, and forward thinking as my mother was at 100."

"I want to bitch more."

"I would like to see all my children and grandchildren happy and healthy."

"I want to be more involved with my children and grandchildren."

"I've thought about going back to work—I volunteer now—but I don't know what exactly where and what it is I want to be doing."

"This is not a rehearsal—at some point you have to take hold

of yourself and ask, 'What is good for me? What makes me happy?'"

"I'm a romantic, and I want life. I don't want to get married, but I want to be on a beach and open the sliding door, and hear the ocean."

"I'm interested in connecting. I am good at networking, and I want to make money doing that."

"People who are happy look forward to the future rather than being pulled back into the past."

To maximize the quality of their lives in the years ahead, our participants were clear that they wanted to continue to be *"engaged."* They acknowledged that it was important to take care of themselves. Many spoke of their exercise program, from walking, to fitness classes, to yoga; this was an active and energetic sample. Some still played tennis, a few in spite of various now-healed or not-quite-healed tennis injuries. They sought engagement with family, friends, and charitable causes. Some pursued new skills or returned to and expanded upon hobbies of earlier years. The general theme seemed to be one of hope and optimism for what lies ahead.

ADVICE FOR THE GENERATIONS WHO FOLLOW

We asked the women in all our groups what they wanted to tell the younger generations. Here is some of their advice:

"Don't look backwards because we can't change things that have already happened; and we can't really look forward, because who knows what will happen. Live in the present."

"Get in touch with what matters; you're left to your own resources; what makes you happy and pleases you...Find it!!"

"Keep a journal."

"Visiting older folks is so important."

"Don't focus on what was—you have to live for what is. Keep going."

"I want to tell younger people you have to enjoy life each day and not put off things until you retire."

"Keep learning, because that will keep you young."

"I would want to tell the generation behind us that you need to spend time getting to know yourself and who you are. You need to realize you can do more than you think you can do."

"The most important thing is to extract the sweetness from life and see the big picture. We know what the stumbling blocks are, but we're moving forward."

Laughter rang out in our discussions as we compared experiences and revealed our foibles. The importance of humor and laughter was evident as a cathartic stress reliever and bonding agent. Our women spoke about the power of humor in their own lives and saw it as perhaps their most important piece of advice for future generations. Laugh. See the funny side of life. One woman put it this way: *"Laughter is healthy for the body and the soul. It actually has a positive effect on heart rate, blood pressure, and breathing."* Others comments about humor included:

"Laugh at the absurdities in life, the ironies, the strange juxtapositions in your world."

"Laugh at yourself; laugh at your mistakes."

"Laugh with children, and share their joy at new discoveries."

"Share a joke and listen to the jokes of others and laugh. If you're like me and can't remember any jokes, laugh at the jokes of others. Laugh at yourself for nor remembering jokes."

"You need to have a sense of humor, because if you don't laugh at some of these things, life can get pretty serious."

And our personal favorite:

"Spend time with upbeat people. Good humor is contagious."

These women were able to laugh at themselves!

"Just after I retired, I was asked out to lunch by my retired friends, and it started to rain. I felt my feet getting wet, and when I looked down, I discovered I had walked out in my bedroom slippers! I went back to work."

"When my hair started turning grey, I tried to use a toner to darken it. My husband would apply the toner, and I felt OK with the process. One evening, we went out to a club, and I wore a purple dress. One of the performers looked at me and said, 'You look great. Your hair matches your outfit!' I was appalled and decided then and there to let my grey and white hair grow in. Now it is my pride and joy and my trademark."

"When I was professor, a young male student would visit me in my office on a regular basis. I told my husband that I thought the boy might have a crush (an innocent crush) on me. Then at his graduation the young man made a point of introducing me to an older woman. 'This,' he said, 'is my grandmother. I always thought you reminded me of her.'"

We tried to keep to the two hours stated in the invitations, but it was clear we could have scheduled the gatherings for at least another couple of hours. When we were asked if we could have a follow-up meeting, we encouraged the women to organize on their own. Some made plans to integrate this theme into an existing book group. We received many email and snail mail thank you notes of gratitude. One said, *"If we meet again in ten years, this will seem like the 'good old days.'"*

CHAPTER THREE

Pulling It All Together

I like not only to be loved but also to be told that I am loved.
The realm of silence is large enough beyond the grave.
This is the world of light and speech.
And I shall take leave to tell you that you are very dear.

George Eliot

Here's our chance to pull it all together, to see from a variety of sources and views what it means to be 70. Can we derive some lessons and useful messages from what we've learned so far? Our theme is certainly one of living long and living well. Are these compatible? If so how? By the end of this chapter we hope you will have a kind of blueprint of life well-lived as represented by the 70Candles women of today.

We saw in the last chapter how eight important themes emerged from our conversation groups: Retirement, Ageism, Functional Changes, Caregiving by this Club-sandwich Generation, Living Arrangements, Social Connections, Grandparenting, and Loss. Leading the list is **retirement**. When to retire? How to retire? And what reason to give self and others for this decision. Our participants were animated as they discussed the passage from work-life to retirement, and emotions ran from ecstatic to terrified to boredom that in at least one case came from *"having too much time on my hands."* Participants revealed the many different ways they anticipated and managed the shift. Pivoting from a previous work life to an uncertain, unstructured future is not always easy and can be fraught with worry. There was no single pattern to follow; each woman had the opportunity to develop, often slowly, her own solution, although some had *"forced retirement"* thrust upon them and others continued to work full-time or more. Some with angst, some with delight, the majority of our participants had already crossed the threshold from busy, scheduled occupations to unstructured free time.

The key to a successful transition appeared to be embracing change imaginatively and with optimism, and having faith in oneself. The women who continued their careers into their 70's knew they would have to cross the threshold eventually, but they continued to find their work meaningful and a critically significant part of their lives. One woman said, *"My mother worked well into her 80's. She is my role model."* Retirement is an issue for each of us, whether it's wondering if we retired too soon, never wanting to retire, or wondering when the time will be right. However, as we've demonstrated above, nearly all the participants in this project who are already retired are making good use of their lives, figuring out how to continue to contribute to society in meaningful ways.

Stereotypical **ageism**, intentional and inadvertent, jolted our women, as they confronted it in their daily lives and in unexpected places. We heard tales about ageism subtle and blatant, at work sites, and in the community. Some anecdotes made us laugh, others elicited chagrin and even anger. Fortunately, we are inspired by exemplary old women everywhere who are having a positive impact on society. Hopefully, we in turn can serve as inspiration for younger generations as they learn to appreciate and respect the amassed wisdom, positive temperament, and the mature problem-solving and mediating skills of senior women. We need to feel pride in ourselves, as well, in the knowledge that we have much of great value to share.

Everyone admitted to **functional changes** that were altering their lives. Some with humor some with worry, some just *"pissed off"* about it. But the women seemed comforted by the fact that they were not alone with their concerns. Our bodies change as we age, even when we eat healthfully, exercise, and try to take good care of ourselves. Sight, hearing, bones, joints, balance, mobility, memory, continence, strength, and stamina—they will never be what they once were—and we might outlive them all! We need to face that fact, access the best and most advanced medical interventions, make the best accommodations we can, and just get on with our lives.

When the conversation turned to **caregiving**, these women of the club-sandwich generation had much to say. They found the strength to take on the role of caretaker for spouse, sibling, and other close relatives, sometimes for years. They knew the strain of illness and the grief of death, and they shared their sadness and their pain. Unspoken were the thoughts of one's own demise…who would take care of the caretakers, and how would our lives end?

Then came another animated conversation about **where to live**. We learned that decisions about where to live as one ages are crucially important for women in their seventies. As they consider geography, extended family, financial matters, the configuration of physical space, access to transportation, and personal comfort and taste, these women are examining the expanding menu of living arrangements available, and making choices they hope will last. We explore the existing range of habitations in more depth in Chapter Five.

We witnessed the power of **social connections**, and especially bonds with women. Their ties to women friends prove to be the greatest support and comfort for those in our groups. Many came to our gathering with a friend, or brought a group of their friends with them. Their advice about the importance of friendships in their lives was heartfelt. Some single, divorced, or widowed women depended on women friends for companionship. Others knew that the odds were that they would outlive their spouses or partners and, ultimately, it would be their friends who would be their *"family."*

Grandparenting was discussed with pride, warmth, delight for those contentedly involved with their grandchildren, but also with some sadness, particularly by those separated geographically from their extended families.

Finally, **loss and death** were emotionally addressed with sadness and poignancy. All admitted that as more and more people we know and love die, we need to face and talk about the last chapter of our own lives.

Given the eight key themes identified above, what are the implications of living long and living well in the 21st century? What is the best we can hope for?

There is much positive literature about aging well, although some of it does not fit well with our own findings. Daniel Levinson for example, in his 1996 book, describes the "seasons of a woman's life" that begins at age 60 and ends at 85 as a time of reflection, a time to reflect upon successes and failures and enjoy the rest of life. He did not meet the women in our study! On the blog, at the conversation groups, and other informal interviews, these women are not sitting down in repose. They are vibrant, energetic, and peppy. They are at the office, at the easel, at the loom, at the gym, playing with their grandchildren, authoring scholarly articles and books, in front of the classroom, on the tennis court, in the courtroom, traveling the world, attending concerts and plays, volunteering their services to help others, and mowing their lawns.

While many women in this study continue to work full or part-time, those who are retired see it as an opportunity to reinvent themselves, in contrast to an article by Price (2000), who suggested that professional women experienced a loss of identity after retirement. The women seemed to fear retirement before the deed was done, and then to relish their newfound opportunities afterwards.

When you ask our 70-year-old women what matters to them, it is the quality of their lives rather the treatment of their infirmities. They do not seem, for example, to want to discuss gait analysis or focus on decay and senescence, as suggested glumly by so much of the typical literature on aging. Terrill and Gullifer interviewed only eight women, but they concluded similarly in 2010 that in their sample the women had a positive outlook on and an acceptance of aging, actually seeing it as a time of freedom.

There are additional parallels between the psychological literature and our project. Seligman's PERMA, for example is a very good way to describe women who are flourishing at 70. When the women in our study reported what is going well for them, positive emotions, engagement, relationships, meaning, and accomplishments were central to their descriptions.

It is time for a new view of 70-year-old women, in particular, and aging, in general; a new image needs to be created. Laura Carstensen calls this the social and biological revolution of our time. Seventy is old. That is a good thing. We can say it with pride. We know from the research literature that a more positive perception of old age will increase both the years we have to live and the quality of those years. We need to re-invent our perceptions of 'aging' and 'old,' as Carstensen implores.

To do this, we can start to celebrate women who thrive and even flourish at 70 years of age and beyond. For example, we received an email about a woman named Marjorie Stoneman Douglas who retired from a successful career as a journalist, only to begin a second career as an environmental spokeswoman, playing an important role in the establishment of the Everglades National Park. The email said, "she continued this career into her 100's and interviewed and spoke until at least 103, and I have seen her in a video at 107. She passed in 1998 at 108."

We're awed by the history of Dr. Ethel Percy Andrus who, after a long career as an educator, and the first female high school principal in the California schools, went on to create the National Retired Teachers Association—the first of its kind—when she was sixty-three. She then went on to found AARP at age seventy-four, running it until age eighty!

You read in our blog section the tale of the energetic woman who late in life began self-publishing books about bridge. She continues playing and writing, even at age ninety-one.

There are so many marvelous stories out there.

We can encourage positive images, even stereotypes, in whatever sphere of influence we operate. A book published by the American Psychological Association in 2005 about women and the media, included only one article about old women, buried way in the back. The author, Kim Kjaersgaard said, "Recent research indicates that images on television continue to celebrate youth and reflect a double standard of aging, with women being more negatively portrayed in the aging process than men." Is this still true? Maybe a little less so today.

Let's hear it for the old at heart!

LIVING LONG

If we women do, indeed, have decades more ahead, we would, of course, like to live them to their fullest. We'd like good health, good spirits, and good times. Advice on sustaining such a long life comes from many sources, and focuses mainly on physical and mental health. Is the spark for longevity mental? physical? genetic? Research continues on all fronts, with much to be learned from those living the longest—the centenarians in our society, who in 2010 numbered about 53,000, but are expected to increase to nearly a million by 2040. The U.S. is home to the largest number of centenarians, and by 2040, 80% are expected to be women!

In the on-going Fordham Centenarian Study, Daniela Joop is exploring the "well-being paradox." In the face of physical decline, losses and life's challenges, why do the very old report feeling happy? Although she agrees that there may be genetic factors at work, Joop comes down on the side of psychological factors making the difference. Her preliminary findings suggest that "those centenarians who appreciate social contact with others, are able to positively reframe difficulties, and find help in religion when confronted with issues, are the ones who value their lives most strongly." It has been hypothesized that in the case of those who do not consider themselves religious, a sense of hope about the future serves the same function.

The chart you'll find in Appendix G summarizes several relevant research projects, including Dan Buettner's 2012 Blue Zone studies, the 2004 international INTERHEART study, Scott's Caring.com blog advice, and Joop's 2010-2012 Centenarian Study.

Blue Zones are named for the blue circles researchers draw on maps, identifying areas of the world where there is unusual longevity. In Ikaria, Greece, for example, one in three islanders lives to be 90, and they have less cancer, cardiovascular disease, depression and dementia than in other parts of Europe. Ikarians are three times more likely to reach age 90 than we in the United States, and the men actually outlive the women. Buettner examined their life-style to see what makes them tick. He describes in detail the Mediterranean diet of these hearty Greeks. They raise their own fresh fruit and vegetables, use antioxidant-rich olive oil liberally, eat honey from their bees that contains anti-inflammatory, anti-cancer, and anti-bacterial properties, bake fresh whole grain bread, and drink wine that is exceptionally rich in polyphenols. Buettner reports that around the world, people who stick to such a diet outlive those who don't by about six years.

In addition to their diet, Ikarians walk wherever they go on their island, getting their exercise through natural activities. They nap in the afternoon, and socialize with family and friends each evening. They don't hurry or watch a clock, and they take time to engage in their religion. They are healthy, energetic, and good-humored. Fresh clean air, crystal clear waters, fresh caught fish to eat. Oh, to live in a Blue Zone!

The INTERHEART study, reported in 2004, included 30,000 people in 52 countries in an effort to identify risks for heart attack. These risks are manageable, and many heart attacks could be avoided, they report, if people controlled smoking, ate a healthy diet that included fruits and vegetables, moderated alcohol consumption, got up off the couch, and obtained medical intervention to help control cholesterol, blood-pressure, diabetes, and obesity.

Scott, at the accessible Caring.com blog site that offers advice and "care for the caregivers," lists questions that if answered in the affirmative, suggest a long life. Five of the items can be controlled by individuals. While the INTERHEART study recommends minimizing anxiety and depression, Scott says it more plainly, "not too much worry."

All agree that it is important to avoid a sedentary life-style. The clear message is, stay as active as possible, and walk whenever and wherever you can. To live a long healthy life, we need to maintain a sensible weight, eat healthfully, stay active, not fret too much, and remain involved with others. We know this. But there's a certain oomph, we think, when research confirms what we know, and when we hear it and read about it anecdotally.

Much current basic scientific research is focused on "positive biology," the search for markers for health and well-being in our genes. Why do some people live to 100 without experiencing chronic diseases?

Important work in the Albert Einstein School of Medicine labs of Dr. Nir Barzilai is focused on the genetic roots of longevity. Barzilai and his team have studied more than 500 New York area healthy centenarians he calls "Superagers." Their subjects are all Ashkenazi Jews from Central Europe, in whom they have identified seven DNA markers that appear to provide protection from common chronic diseases. Correlating with longevity they report, are having a Superager in your family, a small stature, and long telomeres (regions at the end of chromosomes that shorten as you age). Among the critical genetic markers are two copies of CEPT—Cholestrol Ester Transfer Protein—which correlates with slower memory decline, lower risk for dementia, and increased protection against heart disease, with increase in "good" cholesterol.

The good news is that clinical trials are underway for a drug that mimics CEPT. Someday, we might actually be able to take a pill to protect our cardiovascular and cognitive health!

LIVING WELL

So, we see that genes can contribute to longevity; but scientists estimate our genetic make-up accounts for only about 25% of our well-being. The other 75% has to do with how we live.

Rath and Herter describe five universal interconnected elements that shape our lives, derived from a comprehensive Gallup study of people in more than 150 countries. These elements include career, social, financial, physical, and community well-being. Most important is the fact that these elements are interdependent. "Well-being is about the combination of our love for what we do each day, the quality of our relationships, the security of our finances, the vibrancy of our physical health, and the pride we take in what we have contributed to our communities." They report social time to be associated with stress-free happiness. The more social time, the higher the ratio of happiness to stress.

Karl Pillemer, as part of his Cornell Legacy Project, interviewed over 1200 older adults to gather their advice on how to live well. From this group, where the average age was about 80, he derived a list of the ten most important items. They include "live as though life is short," and "happiness is a choice." You can see them all in Appendix H.

George Vaillant offers advice in his book, Aging Well. "Positive aging means to love, to work, to learn something we did not know yesterday, and to enjoy the remaining precious moments with loved ones." Specific qualities that matter he lists as:

1. Future orientation-the ability to plan and hope.

2. The capacity for gratitude and forgiveness.

3. The capacity to love, and to imagine the world as it seems to another.

4. The desire to do things with people.

For graceful aging, Vaillant mentions the qualities listed in our Appendix H chart. He says, "Forgiveness leads to successful aging more often than does nursing old resentments."

Dr. Robert Butler, founding director of the National Institute on Aging, said, in 1975, "In reality, the way one experiences old age is contingent upon physical health, personality, earlier life experience, the actual circumstances of late-life events, and the social support one receives."

Maintaining social connections, having a reason to get up in the morning, minimizing stress and worry, and having a positive outlook, are themes we see repeated throughout the literature. These are qualities we saw reflected in our 70Candles women.

Erik Erikson in 1959 described psychosocial development through eight life stages. The last stage he called "Wisdom." He saw old adults from age 65 up until death as contemplating the lives they had lived and finding wisdom. He was age 57 when he wrote this, and the average life span in America at that time was 74 for White women and 66 for Black women. Erikson was probably not envisioning the increase in longevity in the ensuing 50 years. What might he have imagined for senior adults who looked forward to more evolving ahead? What ego challenges or conflicts does this new generation of old folks face?

As we try to envision this Senior Adult Stage, we have developed a conceptual series of dichotomies and polarities.

1. Active vs Passive

2. Isolated vs Supported

3. Coping vs Giving up

4. Emotional Self vs Professional Self

5. Today vs Long-Term

We know that our group of active women, who for the most part appear to be and say that they are coping successfully, represents just a portion of the spectrum suggested by these polarities. Everyone is not flourishing equally well. We acknowledge that some women become increasingly passive and withdrawn. Some prefer to be alone, even isolated. As illness strikes, even death approaches, the immediate needs of today may conflict with a greater long-term connection with the universe.

As we apply this approach to our blog and conversation groups, we see that women's responses reveal a short-term, immediate, and practical approach to aging, but also a sense of personal history regarding health, memory, and other cognitive functions. An active positive stance toward life predominates. Friendships and social support are in the here-and-now, but the forms and roles they take—daughter, wife, mother, aunt, pal—are historical as well. Actually, at this stage of life, we see that personal identity is often, although not always, more a matter of family and friends than of career and professions. 70Candles women definitely plan for the future—their ninth decade—and they have plenty to say to younger women about flourishing in these senior years.

How do these women spend their time? Let's look at Esther, and see how she makes the most of each day, in this Senior Adult Stage of her life.

ESTHER'S TALE: A Life Well-Lived

Every tale of women who retire from long careers is different. This story is about Esther, a real person, although this is not her name, who seems to encapsulate many available options in one being. She ended a long and successful independent consulting practice rather abruptly, on the day she discovered that her morning yoga class was really more important to her than meeting with a prominent client.

From that moment on, her schedule began to change in a number of ways. Oh, she carried on some of her previous activities, but she became more focused as she set goals to move herself forward. As she had before, Esther filled her time with great attention and energy. She had always multi-tasked—on the phone one could always hear the water running, or pots clanking as she talked—and she kept that up, although it was clear she couldn't juggle quite as many mental activities at one time as she had before.

Esther and her husband had already resettled from their suburban large home to a central city apartment, but the smaller quarters were no deterrent to her entertaining: luncheons to welcome new neighbors, committee meetings of the charitable group she was involved in, holiday dinners for family and friends, all continued without missing a step.

She began her day early with her favorite exercise class and found several hours to practice piano, for that was her personal passion. In between, she served in leading roles on action-oriented committees, attended classes and concerts, met with friends, communicated with her children, spent weekly time with each of her grandchildren, and still cooked nightly dinner for her husband. To reenergize between activities, she found she could substitute ten minute naps for the downward facing dog poses of her younger days. Weekends were a time to relax with her husband, by the sea.

In myriad quiet ways, Esther found ways to enrich the lives of others. She played piano at an assisted living center; she brought her music to the homes of sick and dying friends, and donated her talents at charity auctions. She brought food and solace to friends in need.

When a worker in her apartment building heard her practicing and knocked on her door to ask about the piano, she offered to teach him at no cost, if he would return.

She mentored inner city youth and nurtured her friendships far and near. She shared with all her practice of "gratitude," that she further studied in a class.

Esther's life was not without worry or problems, but she put health issues to the back of her mind and kept moving forward. Every so often she would wonder, "Is this the last carpet I will ever buy?" "The last washing machine?" "The last winter coat?"

Esther: Wife, mother grandmother, musician, involved citizen, social activist, humanist, motivator, and good-hearted woman.

IS THERE A NEW STAGE OF LIFE?

The personal qualities of Esther demonstrate the stage of Generativity that Erikson attributed to psychosocial development during middle adulthood, from about age 40-65: A time to pass along accumulated wisdom and to nurture younger generations. The tasks Erikson posits for mature old age, from about 65 until death, have to do with reflecting back on life, slowing down productivity, and contemplating accomplishments. His wife, Joan Erikson, amended Erikson's theory in 1987 by adding a Ninth Stage of development. That, however, describes the frail old. The women we know seem to fall between these characterizations; perhaps there is now a new Senior Adult Stage to describe.

As the number of years stretch beyond those that Erikson had originally considered, there is now a great deal more to life, especially for women. This "stage of development" has become rich with new possibilities. It's an era of transitions in identity, in daily rhythms, and in the concept of "home." It's a time for reassessment, for acknowledging limitations and health issues, but with resilience, moving forward in spite of them. A time to discover new talents, a time to connect in deeper ways with those we know and love; and a time to contemplate the end of life, for that is surely part of our everyday experience, as we suffer the loss of dear ones and acknowledge our own mortality.

TIME WELL SPENT

Let's step back and briefly speculate—describing our 70Candles woman from a more formal, abstract point of view. This is a shorthand way of assembling our information. We divide our model into two sections, each of which consists of three perspectives or dimensions, as we show in Appendix I and J. This model is probably of most interest to those doing formal or statistical research into aging.

The first section we call *The Challenge of Change*. The first challenge includes a number of issues connected to *identity*—Work outside the home, the homemaker role, and a myriad other social and family concerns. The second challenge is the impact of the aging process on a variety of functions, especially physical well-being, health and illness. The third *Challenge of Change* is how our women are *experienced and perceived by other people*. Issues of ageism arise. They are often the oldest in a social or educational setting, and their age alone often determines the value of their contribution.

The second section of this model is a developmental perspective we call *Growth Over Time*. It is separate to some extent, but also overlaps with many other issues. In a nutshell, it refers to the *past*, the *present*, and the *future*: our yesterdays, todays, and tomorrows.

Taken together, the model provides a blueprint, a schematic picture, of the 70Candles woman in today's world. A part of today is looking ahead. What will life be like for these women at the end of their eighth and into their ninth decade of existence?

Advice to younger women, the wisdom of yesterday, we base on a specific question asked in the groups. "What do think is important for younger women to know?"

When we were younger, our attitudes about aging and longevity were influenced by our role models. Now our own future outlook affects our attitudes, which in turn influence how we cope with life. When we believe that we create our own happiness, we inject optimism and humor into life, and more positive experiences are likely, while pessimism and negativity can contribute to a cup-half-empty existence.

There's so much more to learn about women living in their eighth decade. It would be interesting, for example, to collect more specific demographic and lifestyle information from respondents. Vaillant and other researchers were able to come to significant conclusions by knowing the alcohol use, sleep patterns, weight, exercise regimens, and so on, of their participants. There is much to consider here.

Future studies of elder women must employ larger samples, different group formats, and wider inquiry. Our participants were mostly middle-class, well-educated women who do not have to worry about their next meal or having a roof over their heads. Our participants, to some extent were racially diverse, but not nearly diverse enough. Long term, longitudinal projects will tell us if the 70Candles women's self-predictions of their future lives came true, or whether intervening and unexpected events altered the course of their expectations.

There are many topics mentioned, but not covered in depth in our groups, topics that are important now and will matter to us more in the decades ahead. We will explore some of these rapidly evolving issues in the final chapter, including the range of senior living options, the role of advancing technology in our lives, new transportation choices, ways to spend our time, and embracing death as a part of our life span. For now it is reasonable to conclude that a positive and optimistic stance toward life's struggles and challenges, and a concerted effort to both establish and maintain social connections, will steady the course of even the worst of times. This is a message we heard repeatedly from our respondents.

Now let's look at what experts have said about these matters.

CHAPTER FOUR

What Do the Experts Say?

A good life with twists and turns like the river.
Maureen Sze

When we began this project, we looked to the published literature on aging to learn how women in their eighth decade define themselves and thrive. We knew we were in the first generation of professional women en masse who have defined ourselves by our work and are now beyond the traditional age of retirement. Each day we're bombarded by newspaper articles, magazine spreads, new popular books, and widely distributed leaflets describing life's challenges, dangers, and options in our old age. To inform ourselves in a more systematic way about women and aging, we turned both to books written for a general audience—old favorites and recent additions—and to the scholarly literature. Here is a brief taste of what we found, beginning more or less chronologically with books and moving on to journal articles and research studies.

Simone de Beauvoir's 1972 book, *The Coming of Age,* is a grand tome that scrupulously details the problems associated with growing old. Just as her 1949 book *The Second Sex* became the foundational tract that launched contemporary feminism, *The Coming of Age* introduces us to another "other" as she turns her activist energies from women, in general, to older adults. De Beauvoir traces the history of attitudes toward aging, from ancient times forward, and expresses outrage at society's poor treatment of older adults in her country, France, in the 1950's, presenting a fierce call to action against the marginalization of the aging. Still relevant today? We think so.

She blamed societal attitudes and the government's poor social services for the ill treatment of seniors who were removed from society and placed in badly run and unsightly institutions, where they languished without stimulation or attention. She felt that in these settings their dignity was destroyed and their lives shortened by poverty and ill-health, causing an overall rapid decline. De Beauvoir felt strongly, "if old age is not to be an absurd parody of our former life"...we must "go on pursuing ends that give our existence meaning—devotion to individuals, to groups, or to causes, social, political, intellectual or creative work."

In 1986, Erikson, Erikson, & Kivnick published *Vital Involvement in Old Age*. True to its title, the authors promote the need for older adults to remain engaged and focused on the present. The book's strength is a review and elaboration of Erik Erikson's well-known eight-stage life cycle, with a focus on the last stage of life, old age. The final chapter offers reflections on and suggestions for "vital involvement."

In *The Fountain of Age*, published in 1993, Betty Friedan explores the frontier of old age from her view as a woman then in her sixties. Our age mates remember Friedan as the woman who launched "second-wave feminism" in the 1960's with *The Feminine Mystique* (do you remember the now classic "problem without a name?"). Thirty years later she chronicles the lives of already liberated, accomplished women, as they find new energy through the aging process. Ever in the vanguard of the social and political thought of her time, Friedan examines a variety of aspects of aging, highlighting the ways people continue to grow and live with vitality. Through personal interviews and discussions, she demonstrates that there is, indeed, much more to longevity than the medical deteriorations so focused on by stereotypical gerontology. Those she interviews describe ways they've discovered to reinvent themselves, to create new challenges and adventure. She notes how they respond to others with a new, more honest and genuine voice.

Friedan sees wisdom, compassion, sensitivity, and flexibility as "unique strengths that can emerge in age…if we don't measure ourselves against the standards of youth." She suggests that "free from the old rigid boundaries that once defined work, the fountain of age opens possibilities of change and life that need have no limits." We love even the idea of a "fountain of age!"

Letty Cottin Pogrebin's 1996 book *Getting Over Getting Older* presents an intimate and frank pre-curser to the 70Candles women— the book could be renamed "Celebrating Getting Older!" She describes a complex portrait of the latter part of Middle Age—from roughly ages 50-65 and beyond—and notes how little had been studied about that cohort of women at that time. After conversations, interviews, and group discussions with her 50 year-old peers, she concludes that caring, compassion, and kindness become critical. The "need to be needed" and Erikson's term, "generativity," capture what she observes as the crux of good guidance to the next generation.

Pogrebin herself values productive, active, and positive use of her time, and she sees others demonstrating a similar energy in work, volunteerism, new learning, travel, and the nurture of both old and new relationships. Our 70Candles women echo Pogrebin's reluctance to become invisible and "retiring," with their positive and active stance and their engagement with life. Her view of middle age contrasts sharply with the identical years—decades ago called old age—which were marked by physical infirmities and death.

Daniel Levinson's *The Seasons of a Woman's Life*, also published in 1996, makes an equally important contribution to our topic, but for a very different reason, as you will see. Based on in-depth interviewing of 45 women born between 1935 and 1947 (one-third homemakers, one-third business women, one-third academics), Levinson develops a ladder of development, as he did earlier for men. He concludes that there are four separate and distinct seasons in life. The season relevant to our project is "late adulthood," ages 60-85, which Levinson describes as a time to reflect upon successes and failures and enjoy the rest of life. Considering the active and continuingly productive lives the majority of our 70Candles women live, we suspect they would vehemently disagree with Levinson's description of their stage of life. But he does confirm a certain stereotype, and for this reason it seems important to consider his work.

Joan M. Erikson, in 1997, proposed a Ninth Stage of development to extend the eight Eriksonian psychological stages posited by her husband. She describes the central challenge of this Ninth Stage as "integrity vs. despair." Integrity, the coherence and wholeness in the older adult, is connected to wisdom. Despair is its antithesis. Without integrity and wisdom, the late 80's into one's 90's, typically marked by the body losing autonomy, would also be a time of despair and depression.

This is relevant to our project because, as we saw in the previous chapter, it is possible that another stage or phase of lifelong development, a Senior Adult Stage, precedes this depiction of old-old age. Remember, American adults are living longer than ever before, and they are working later in life. Medical care for seniors has expanded, and social conditions such as choices of living arrangements have multiplied. These factors suggest the Senior Adult Stage may be a time of part-time or even continued full-time work, volunteering, and care-taking—a period of active, positive engagement with life and family and society. Physical decline and a preoccupation with health and medical issues would come later. So, too, would come a time of reflection and assessment of one's past—a more static rather than dynamic time of life reminiscent of Levinson's description of the older adult.

A good guess now is that a Senior Adult Stage coincides roughly with the ages of 65 to one's early 80's, and an Old Age stage from one's middle or late 80's into the 90's and further. Age and stage are never in perfect harmony—witness people who are old at 40 or young at 70!

Cathleen Rountree, a visual artist, photographer, and writer, has written a series of "decade books" celebrating women at 40, 50, 60, and *On Women Turning 70: Honoring the Voices of Wisdom*. This is a lovely, inspirational book with beautiful photographs and interviews of 16 women, some who are famous, such as Betty Friedan and Doris Lessing, and some who are not. Although it lacks ethnic diversity, this is more than just a picture book to display on a living room table.

George Vaillant's 2002 *Aging Well* is worth reading and re-reading for the eloquence of its writing, the rich stories of real lives, and the profound insights about growing old with grace and joy. Vaillant invites readers to master three tasks in order to achieve a satisfying old age. They are "Generativity," "Keeper of the Meaning," and "Integrity." "Generativity" provides the foundation for a successful old age. Vaillant defines it as putting "into the world more than was there before." Synonyms might be creativity, accomplishment, and caring. "Keeper of the Meaning" has to do with character and social justice, preserving the past but not in a rigid way. "Integrity" is the final stage, the task of the very old according to Vaillant and Erik Erikson. Vaillant suggests that to achieve positive aging, even despite disability, we focus on human dignity, and adopt an almost Buddhist response to life.

Laura Carstensen's 2009 *A Long Bright Future* is full of good practical advice from a longtime longevity researcher from Stanford. Carstensen says her goal in writing the book is to help reinvent old age, which she sees as the social and biological revolution of our time. She includes information about Social Security, technology, Medicare, and more, and is writing with the bottom-line premise that more and more people are living to be centenarians—more than one million by 2050.

In another 2009 book of note, *The Third Chapter: Passion, Risk, and Adventure in the 25 Years After 50*, Lightfoot-Lawrence, a Harvard sociologist, interviewed 40 women and men between 50 and 75. Basing her work, as many others continue to do, on that of life-span theorist Erik Erikson, she explores how those aging successfully develop many ways to funnel their energy, skills and passions into new areas of growth.

More recent works include gerontologist Karl Pillemer's 2011 book, *30 Lessons for Living: Tried and True Advice from the Wisest Americans*, resulting from his Cornell Legacy Project. Interviewees, average age about 80, provide their best advice to younger people. And in 2012, *Retiring But Not Shy: Feminist Psychologists Create their Post Careers*, Ellen Cole (yes, this book's co-author) and Mary Gergen (this book's editor) brought to the printed page 21 trailblazing professional women who are considering or experiencing retirement, each in her unique way.

Finally, the theoretical physicist Michio Kaku gives us a compelling glimpse into the future. In his very readable and enlightening book from 2012, *Physics of the Future: How Science Will Shape Human Destiny and Our Daily Lives by the Year 2100*, Kaku examines cutting edge research projects around the world and describes the exploding pace of advances in computer sciences, biotechnology, genetics, telecommunications, robotics, artificial intelligence, and nanotechnology, and the impact of these on people's lives. Kaku paints a picture of the world of tomorrow, but amazingly, as we read our daily newspapers and scan the web, we see that some of his predictions are happening right now. A sick boy attends school from his bed, through a robot in his classroom. In fact, robots abound. Incredibly, the world robot population is currently estimated to be about 8.6 million. Stem cell researchers have begun to create human organs in the laboratory. Even our food may be created in a laboratory, from stem cells of animals. Meals might be produced on 3-D printers. Surgeries of the future may be incision-free using complicated ultrasound devices. Some of this work is already here.

Sick Granny Studies. Our search of scientific studies began as we typed "70 year-old women" into Google Scholar. We found, "Balance training in 70-year-old women," "Periodontal conditions in 70-year-old women with osteoporosis," "Epidemiology of osteoporosis and osteoporotic fractures," "Cost effectiveness of Simvastatin treatment to lower cholesterol levels in patients with coronary heart disease," and "Informed choice in mammography screening: A randomized trial of a decision aid for 70-year-old women." Now these are important topics, to be sure, but the array suggested a predominance of health related issues in the scholarly literature. It seemed the first response by many researchers to the thought of a 70 year-old woman was in the realm of failing physical function, dementia, or decisions about medication.

To focus on psychology, the PsycInfo website was the logical next step. Here we found under "70 year-old women"—"Interventions to increase physical activity among aging adults," "Effectiveness of Tai Chi as a therapeutic exercise in improving balance and postural control," "Evidence-based guidelines for cardiovascular disease prevention in women: 2007 Update," and "The potential of gait analysis to contribute to differential diagnosis of early stage dementia." Grimmer, still.

Then, a check of the American Psychological Association's Committee on Aging (at apa.org). Their concerns, not inappropriately to be sure, were "dementia guidelines," "quality health care," and "family caregivers."

One might conclude that the general public, the health care industry, and even psychologists view issues of relevance to 70 year-old women as either medical or pharmacological.

It occurred to us at this point that a fitting title for this book might be "Look at all the pills on Granny's nightstand!" But wait. What about a more *positive* direction? We wondered if the emerging field of Positive Psychology might help us on our quest to learn about women thriving and flourishing at age 70 and beyond. As you will see, it was there that we actually found quite a bit.

Discovering Positive Psychology. Traditional psychology, since its inception, focused on what is wrong with people and how psychologists might help to right the wrongs. Significant progress was made in understanding and treating numerous psychological disorders, such as depression, anxiety, and phobias. However, while alleviating suffering, much of psychology neglected to examine what is right with people.

In 1998 Martin E. P. Seligman, then president of the American Psychological Association, proposed a new approach, to study that which enhances a life worth living. The idea was not to replace traditional psychology, but to augment it. Positive Psychology is grounded in the belief that people want to lead meaningful and fulfilling lives, to cultivate what is best within themselves, to enhance their experiences of love, work, and play. In the past decade and a half the field has mushroomed, creating a science that also builds strengths that enable people to achieve the best things in life. We discovered that terms such as "life satisfaction," "subjective well-being," "resilience," "happiness," "thriving," "optimism," and "gratitude" now abound in the scientific and popular presses.

In Seligman's 2011 book, *Flourish,* he introduces the concept of PERMA, the basic elements of life satisfaction: Positive Emotion, Engagement, Relationships, Meaning, and Accomplishment. It is largely through the lenses of these five elements that later in this book, we examine the lives of 70-year old women today.

Positive Aging

Here is a quick look at some of the conclusions about positive aging:

- Personality, social and cognitive characteristics are relatively stable through adulthood and old age.
- Intimate relationships affect how we age.
- Older adults have higher levels of marital satisfaction.
- Aging is a time of freedom for choices to remain busy, productive and creative, even in retirement.
- Higher levels of self-compassion lead to fewer negative responses related to specific life events, such as retirement.
- Life satisfaction, gratitude towards a God, and resilience in the face of adversity are key factors in aging.
- As we age, stress and anger steeply decline and psychological well-being increases.

George Vaillant, succinctly tells us, "Aging happy and well, instead of sad and sick is at least under some personal control."

Successful Aging: How is it Described? Despite Bowling and Dieppe's admonition in 2005 that any definition of successful aging should "include elements that matter to elderly people" themselves, we found that most definitions in fact have more to do with the academic discipline of the investigator. Biomedical models emphasize the "absence of disease," for example, and psychosocial models emphasize life satisfaction. Lay views emphasize such topics as personal growth, continued learning and giving, financial security, and physical appearance.

A 2013 article by Johnson and Mutchler, "The Emergence of a Positive Gerontology: From Disengagement to Social Involvement," takes the reader on a journey through the field of positive psychology as it relates to the study of aging. The authors focus first on the gloomy past and then move to the bright and optimistic future of the literature. They "highlight three interconnecting examples of a positive gerontology: successful aging, productive aging, and civic engagement in later life."

More specifically, in 1990 Smith and van der Meer concluded that creativity is a key to positive aging, finding that "elderly women" who were creative were also emotionally flexible. They demonstrated less negative attitudes toward aging, and they were less defensive about illness. In 2005 Friedman and colleagues examined the relationship between social engagement and quality and length of sleep, finding social relationships and good sleep to be protective factors against disease.

Wink and Helson, using data from a longitudinal study of women ("the Mills cohort"), concluded, interestingly, that practical wisdom, defined by such qualities as empathy, understanding, and maturity in relationships, "increases from young adulthood to mature middle age." This was most notably true for women in certain occupations, such as psychotherapy, and women who had experienced traumatic events, such as divorce.

Those who have investigated recovery from illness and disorders have found that there were reliable relationships between life satisfaction and a multitude of character strengths such as gratitude, bravery, creativity, love of learning, appreciation of beauty, humor, and kindness. These characteristics may, alternatively, constitute a really good definition of optimal aging when evaluating how older adults cope and manage adversity within their lives.

Exploring resilience, researchers have continued to question how older adults are still able to display normalcy and personal growth despite extreme adversity. In the past, and still today as we've noted, older adulthood has been viewed as a time of decline and the accumulation of negative life events (e.g., widowhood, the diagnosis of chronic disease). Many would assume that older adults are unhappy and unable to successfully cope with these transitions, but current researchers have proven this wrong! Although professionals and society in general may have specific views on grief and the process of bereavement, many individuals who lose a significant other, for example, display great resilience.

Retirement. Retirement is a key issue for us and our female age-mates. Ellen Goodman, the Pulitzer Prize winning columnist and one of the first women to open up the op-ed pages to women writers, expressed her own ambivalence on the matter. She wrote in her farewell column, "I wish I could find the right language to describe this rite of passage. Retirement, that swoon of a word, just won't do." And "The Spanish translation, jubilación, is a bit over the top for our own mix of feelings."

Due to the upsurge in numbers of working women that began in the 1970s, women are now experiencing their own retirement directly, rather than indirectly through their husbands. In 2011 Frieze, Olson, and Murrell looked at retirement decision-making by currently employed women and men with MBA degrees. The women who were sure they wanted to work past age 65 were non-traditional in their gender-role attitudes and found value in their work. If they were married they expected that their husbands, too, would continue to work past age 65.

In interviews of 28 retired professional women, Price concluded that the women experienced loss of social contacts and professional challenges and, above all, lost their sense of identity. They also grappled with negative stereotypes about retirees. While these women began retirement with ease and high expectations, they relatively quickly began to "experience difficulty adjusting to the loss of their professional role," much as we've seen for many years in the male retirement literature.

On the other hand there are also stories of thriving retirees. George Vaillant in *Aging Well* notes that retirement allowed "septuagenarian women like Mary Elder free to be creative once more." At 75 she became the editor of a small newspaper. Another published her first "serious book" at 65, and so on. Vaillant describes this phenomenon as "concrete evidence that creativity remains a possibility in late life" and concludes with the upbeat note: "Retirement should be at least as much fun as fourth grade."

Positive Interventions. A Positive Intervention is an activity—one might call it a "treatment modality" with a twist—that aims to increase positive emotions and life satisfaction. We think of an intervention as positive if its goal is more than symptom reduction, more for example than asking a person with anxiety to breathe deeply and slowly. One good example is a program we came upon called Mindful Self-Compassion, created to help increase an individual's well-being through the "construction" of self-compassion. The activities from this program help older adults redefine how they treat themselves when going through difficult times and help facilitate a self-compassionate mindset that aims to improve overall well-being.

Originally, we considered calling this section on Positive Interventions "Sex, Drugs, and Rock 'n' Roll," since the first interventions we found, truly, were about the positive effects of sex, moderate alcohol consumption, and music. Further exploration of articles and chapters, however, revealed a broader, albeit less zingy list of possible positive interventions for use with aging women. The following is a quick summary:

- Improvements in varied cognitive skills are possible for seniors.
- Resistance training produces cognitive benefits.
- Moderate alcohol consumption improves cognitive functioning and a sense of subjective well-being. (Good news for those of us who like our glass of wine with dinner!)
- Music enhances identity, self-understanding, connections with others, and a sense of well-being for seniors.
- Positive self-perceptions of aging can prolong life expectancy

One fascinating 2002 study by Yale epidemiologists Levy, Slade, Kunkel, and Kasl, found that "individuals with more positive self-perceptions of aging, *measured up to 23 years earlier* [emphasis ours], lived 7.5 years longer than those with less positive perceptions of aging." Given that positive self-perceptions about aging in young adulthood can apparently prolong life expectancy, we are well-advised to encourage and broadcast positive stereotypes of the old and older. There are many models throughout the world of elevated status of old people. Alaska Natives, for example, revere their elders in small and large ways every day. On a broader scale, we agree with the Yale epidemiologists, who admonish us to end the "societally sanctioned denigration of the aged." Old is beautiful. The 70Candles project is a small step in this effort.

CONCLUSION

Here are some facts to keep in mind. It's widely known that the United States experienced an explosion of births after American soldiers returned home from World War II, and it is those born between January 1, 1946 and December 31, 1964 that sociologists and the U.S. Census Bureau call "baby boomers." On January 1st of the year 2011, the very first baby boomers turned 65; in 2016 they will turn 70. The U. S. Census Bureau's Population Division currently estimates the number of baby boomers to be 78.2 million. It is estimated that in

2016, 7,918 will turn 70 each day, 330 each hour. By 2050, the number of people who live to be 100 is expected to reach a phenomenal million. In fact, it is estimated that in 2014 over 53,000 people in the U.S. alone have already reached the 100 mark.

Do these statistics give our generation of pre-baby boomers— sometimes called the silent generation, or the lucky few—a mandate to learn what we can about thriving as elders in order to pave the way for those who follow? We thought so when we began this project, but it quickly became apparent that this sense of responsibility toward the baby boomers was not widely shared by our peers. Our women concluded that this project has benefits for us, now. And the 'now' is urgent. We pre-boomer career women reached and passed "retirement age" without role models. For example, a graduate student at Harvard University in the early 1960s had only one female professor, and that professor did not get tenure. Many of us were advised by our parents and counselors to become teachers, nurses, or secretaries, certainly not engineers or physicians. In 1971 it was noted that there were only a tiny proportion of college women who go on to get Ph.D.'s in any discipline.

The presence of women among doctoral recipients has increased markedly since the 1960s. By 1996 we're told by the *American Psychologist* that 62% of those completing doctoral degrees in psychology were women. Other professional fields, such as law and medicine, experienced similar seismic shifts; ours is indisputably the generation that began to change the landscape for professional women.

So it turns out that there is a great deal written, after all, about positive aging. We have presented just the tip of the proverbial iceberg, for as the boomers move past retirement, more is being written with each passing week. New studies, creative concepts, and a rapidly changing future lie ahead.

While there are many paths to describing successful aging, some of which we've outlined above, there do seem to be some clear common denominators across studies. In the realm of physical well-being, avoiding tobacco, moderate use of alcohol, maintaining a healthy weight, regular exercise, and sufficient sleep are well-known factors across the life-span and also clearly documented in the research on aging. The psychological realm emphasizes creativity, a stable intimate relationship, being active, social engagement, continued learning, and giving, as factors that both promote and describe successful aging.

We've learned what our 70Candles women have to say. Did the Blogs and our Discussion Group format suggest new styles of aging and different approaches to the 8th decade of life and beyond? Or did we confirm and substantiate prior ideas and recommendations? Maybe both. This look at the past provides a perfect springboard to the future as we present it in the chapter ahead.

CHAPTER FIVE

What Lies Ahead?

Aging is not 'lost youth' but
a new stage of opportunity and strength.

Betty Friedan

Thirty more years of life is statistically possible for women in their seventies today. Many wonder what lies ahead, if they qualify for that gift of time. How to live it? What to give? What to ask for? What might life be like in the future?

Several important topics move to the foreground, including where to live and how to get about. Women try to imagine what they will do with that stretch of time, whether or not they can keep up with technological advances, how they will to manage changes in body and health. And ultimately, they worry about loss, and the end of life.

There is some urgency in these questions, for society in general, for women now in their seventies, and for the millions of aging boomers. According to the Social Security Administration, the average life span is 86 for women now 65; by 2050, one in five Americans will be "seniors," over 65. How will this nation adjust to this rapidly shifting demographic?

WHERE TO LIVE?

The important question of living arrangements weighs on the minds of most of women as they get older. For those who have been married, with children, the large family house becomes too big, too expensive to maintain, and its stairs become a challenge. Women, especially if they are on their own, have to determine the right time to move and where to live next. Choices include whether to live alone, join a community of age-mates, or move in with children or other relatives. Perhaps they settle near other family members. Questions arise as to what happens to old relationships and familiar places that may be left behind.

Nursing homes were once the primary choice for families seeking care for elderly parents. But the outcome in nursing homes was problematic. When seniors didn't have a say in that choice, they became depressed and inactive, and died. Such institutionalization sped the decline of memory and hastened disorientation and confusion. Friedan describes the "self-fulfilling prophesy of decline" that pervaded this society, as she observed old people in the 1980's.

Today, 21st century models of community living and helpful technological innovations abound. In response to the concerns women in their seventies have about living arrangements, we review here the options that currently exist in this country, and we note some emerging patterns.

An American woman in her seventies is likely to outlive/or outgrow her partner. A healthy scenario could include the following: Single, widowed, or divorced, she is on her own, but not isolated. Because maintaining a sense of community is of great importance to her, she is open to new encounters. Intentional and unintentional linkages and associations sprout wherever she spends her time. Her network of friends and acquaintances includes men, women, and children of all ages. They are family members, neighbors, familiar faces in her local stores, in her health club, fellow parishioners, travel companions, and members of her interest groups. Even if she moves to a new location, it is their support that helps her thrive.

Aging in Place

Many women want to live in their own home indefinitely. Davis tells us, "Almost 90 percent of Americans 65 or older plan to stay in their homes as they age." They feel comfortable in familiar surroundings, they know their neighbors, and treasure old friendships and ties that have endured for decades. Social connections are the key ingredients in any living choices made; and there is a safety factor to consider. Familiar neighbors, local merchants, the mail carrier, and delivery people in established neighborhoods can usually be counted on to keep an eye on the more vulnerable citizens.

Essential elements for aging in place include community infrastructure with coordinated resources and adequate transportation options. Also important is Universal home design incorporating assistive technology that can reduce risk, be cost effective, and create connections to the world beyond the home. Municipalities across the country are designing projects to help older adults continue to live in their homes and communities (www.CIAP.org). There is an ongoing U.S. Senate effort to amend and update the Older Americans Act. When it was reauthorized by Congress in 2006, it mandated the creation of Area Agencies on Aging. One aspect of the Act, The Community Innovations for Aging in Place Initiative, provides grants and technical support to communities across the country to create collaborative projects that serve a broad spectrum of activities. The Atlanta Regional Commission, for example, has created a long-term plan for 14 regional Lifelong Communities (www.atlantaregional.com/aging-resources). By 2030, over one in five of Atlanta's residents would be over 60, and there was much work to be done to prepare for them. The plan provides assessment tools, with a focus on integration of older adults into communities rather than segregating them.

As people voice their preference for "aging in place," surrounded by the familiar, government support is turning toward home-care in place of large scale institutional accommodations. Modern technology is providing safety measures that never existed before: Twenty-four hour help systems, mobile phones, surveillance cameras, and GPS locators. Through new technologies, supportive loved ones can also help monitor the safety and security of older adults.

Universal Design suggests ways to make any living environment safe and accessible, for people of all ages. Originated by James Joseph Pirkl, it is intended as proactive planning to last a lifetime. Its features are now included in many new homes, even for young people, but need to be retro-fitted in older dwellings. Conveniences throughout the home include absence of steps at entries, wide doorways that can accommodate a walker or a wheelchair, slip-resistant flooring, lever-style door knobs, adjustable remote controlled lighting fixtures, walk-in showers, hands-free toilets, space under kitchen counters for seating, and side-by-side refrigerators. Railings for support, along with ramps and lifts, can be added as needed.

Urban Intentional Communities

Many retirees are drawn back to cities, where public transportation, walkability and abundant services are offered. In New York and Philadelphia, women in 70Candles conversation groups described selling the home where they raised their families, and moving back to "the city." The enticement of urban living with amenities just outside your door, is strong. In response to the enormous increases in their aging populations, many American cities have started to make changes in their urban landscape. They must hurry to keep up with this surge. They acknowledge that social connections are the key ingredients in any living choices made, and are making a range of efforts to address that. Philadelphia has a task force examining ways to make the city more accessible and attractive to older folks. They are promoting more walkable communities. Projects like Friends in the City, have a full calendar, generated by the group members, with options galore, in the company of like-minded peers. Women in 70Candles groups expressed how important that was to them.

> *"I just have to step outside, and there always something to do."*

> *"I walk everywhere. It's the way I explore the city and it is also my exercise."*

Philadelphia's non-profit Friends in the City-FitC/FCC (www. friendscentercity.org) calls itself a "community without walls," with a mission "to bring its members closer to the resources of our city and to one another." It offers daily programs for residents of urban apartments with every cultural taste…hiking, public parks, museums, special speakers, exploration of various ethnic restaurants, concerts, theatre, book clubs, play readings, travel, a morning coffee klatch, and volunteering in the community.

The Transition Network's Caring Collaborative (www.thetransitionnetwork.org) specifically for women over 50, in New York and many other urban areas, does many of the same things. TNN proposes, "through programs, events and small group interaction…to inspire and support each other [through] a life of learning, engagement and leadership." They call this an "intentional community," as they take advantage of existing facilities and partnerships. Women help each other, gather socially, and are at the other end of a phone in time of need. Aging Improvement Districts in New York City intend to help older people "live as independently and engaged in the city as possible." New York has begun to use idle school buses to transport seniors to do their grocery shopping during the day. In East Harlem's "aging improvement district," merchants have increased the size of the type so signs are easier to read, and they have set out folding chairs so seniors can rest as they shop.

Ashby Village, in the Berkeley area, is another such community network, organized to provide supportive resources that will allow their members to remain in their homes as they get older (www.av.clubexpress.com). In such collaborative efforts, services provided by community members or outside sources can include home repair and remodeling, light housekeeping, grocery shopping, Meals on Wheels, to name only a few.

Other Possibilities

For those who move out of the old homestead, but not to a city center, there are numerous other options. Some women move in with their children, or to homes nearby. Other possibilities include General Community Housing for independent living, Lifestyle Housing, as in Active Adult Communities, or Co-Housing, that creates its own community. These have no inherent services included, but would benefit from Aging in Place initiatives and supports as residents age. Service enriched housing includes Assisted Living, Continuing Care Communities, or if needed, skilled nursing facilities.

Moving in with the Family

Some families prepare well ahead for incorporating a grandma into their homes. Some build a "mother-in-law apartment" onto the house, retro-fit a garage, or have a separate floor allocated for a grandparent's residence. When this works well, grandparents can have the pleasures of being near grandchildren as they grow, the children can profit from knowing their grandparents more intimately, and their parents can be available if the elder needs assistance. As a bonus, families might have a built-in baby sitter. In some ethnic groups this is an expected arrangement, and the grandmother may assume cooking and other household tasks, if she is not otherwise occupied.

Home Sharing

Women on their own are experimenting with home sharing in cities across the country. Several women purchase a large home together and work out legal, financial, and social sharing protocols, thus forming a small community, while reducing their individual living expenses. Some cities and states have created on-line services that link people with similar needs: in Oregon, "Let's Share Housing," in Vermont, "Home Share Now." Although reports of these arrangements describe women still employed, some are likely to extend through retirement years, as well.

An on-line matching service for women, Roommates4Boomers. com analyzes participants' questionnaires to suggest compatible living companions.

Retirement Communities

Co-Housing

Co-housing is a model for adults 50 or older, brought to the States from Denmark by architects McCamant and Durrett. It is a collaborative venture wherein the residents participate in designing and operating their own neighborhoods. At the social center is usually a common house containing a large kitchen, dining area, and communal recreation sites that might include a meeting area, a library, a laundry, and a playground. In this setting, neighbors can meet informally and share in regularly scheduled group dinners and community events (www.eldercohousing.org). The co-housing model harkens back to communes of the 60's, and their focus on interdependence. There are currently 205 such communities in various stages of development in the U.S., listed in the on-line cohousing directory, with 109 considered "completed" (www.cohousing.org/directory/view21478). Some of these intentional communities are multi-generational, while a few are planned strictly for elders. They are ecologically minded, and many produce food on their communal lands.

The Elders Guild of Berkeley California is one such group exploring avenues to creating affordable senior co-housing. Their motto is, "Conscious Aging for the Greater Good." Their mission is to "reimagine our old age, look after one another and embody wisdom that will enable us to heal the future." Inspiration came from the work of Rabbi Zalman Schacter-Shalomi, and his book *From Aging to Sageing* (www.meetup.com/Aging-In-Community/events/48185642/).

Independent Living

An example of a growing independent living venture is Philadelphia's Friends Center City Riverfront, a condominium project developed by a non-profit Quaker group. Its goal is to help older people remain independent, within a supportive community, while they stay involved in downtown Philadelphia—their campus and playground. Health care support is available here.

Retirement Communities, with no health care included, cater to those over age 55. Across the country, these might appear as multi-story apartment buildings, as sprawling condominiums, or as homes on golf courses. Whether singular structures or entire villages, these planned communities offer an array of amenities, activities, and services for a newer, more energetic senior generation. Newspaper ads herald the "invigorating atmosphere," "with just the right vibe," and declare that "getting old isn't what it used to be." A visit to a new suburban retirement village reveals a scene that is a cross between a country club and a summer camp. Attractive homes line the edges of a golf course. A grand clubhouse is replete with spaces for card-playing, art studios, a large fitness center, and a swimming pool. People are actively involved in all manner of activities. Outdoors, some are biking, some are playing tennis, while others are on the golf course. The newsletter lists the dozens of clubs offered, including those that focus on sports, crafts, intellectual discussions, books, politics, volunteer opportunities, religious affiliations, and travel.

Other Independent living arrangements, where activities are not typically provided, are referred to as senior housing, senior homes, or senior apartments. In a wide range of settings, from basic apartment houses to upscale resort-like accommodations, seniors can live as independently as possible within a community of peers, knowing that if support services are not available, they can acquire them on their own when and if they are needed. Some independent living arrangements are part of a larger step-down scheme that includes assisted living and long-term care facilities when needed.

Assisted Living

For those who need assistance with daily care, Assisted Living apartments, and more recently small Assisted Living boarding homes may be the right fit. Here, nurse aids or technicians can offer help with activities of daily living including meals, dressing, toileting, and medication. Transportation is available for group outings and recreational purposes. Many assisted living facilities are embedded in Continuing Care Communities where step-down or step-up possibilities exist as health conditions dictate. Residents can move from independent living to assisted living, and if necessary, to an adjacent skilled nursing facility, or back again as their situation improves.

Long-Term Care

Even the once-dreaded nursing home is undergoing evolutionary changes. The Eden Alternative (www.edenalt.org), conceived of by geriatrician Dr. William Thomas (2004) to ward off the suffering he saw caused by loneliness, helplessness, and boredom, incorporates nature, animals, children, and increased human interactions into the traditional nursing home setting. His newer model, The Green House Project (http://changingaging.org) advances the comfort and humanizes the experience further. It proposes "small intentional communities for groups of elders and staff, to focus on living full and vibrant lives" (www.thegreenhouseproject.org). There are no standard schedules to follow, and no more than 12 "elders" live in each home. Each has a private room with bath near a commons area that includes a kitchen, living room, and large communal dining table. There are more than 140 of these nonprofit nursing homes, in 24 states, with dozens more in development at the time of this writing. They are staffed by nursing assistants who participate in all aspects of the elders' day.

Dr. Marc Agronin, in his book *How We Age,* describes the rich human lessons he has learned from the old people in the Miami Jewish Health system, where he has been the long- standing psychiatrist, providing mental health support to the residents of its large nursing home. He quotes a lively woman who remained a resident after her sick husband died, and who continued to participate with other women, with great energy. She said it was like being on a cruise ship. No bed to make and plenty to do.

MOVING OUT AND MOVING ON

The first step in changing residences is, of course, moving, often fraught with resistance, nostalgia, sadness, and even fear. The family home is filled with memories of an earlier life. Moving from a large home to any smaller residence often entails sifting through a lifetime of memorabilia, choosing what to discard and what to bring forward. So much "stuff" accumulated over the years. Difficult choices to make, as one chapter ends and the next begins. Relinquishing personal items can feel like a loss of one's history. However, once accomplished, many find that new vistas can open.

New professions have emerged to assist in this complicated process. Personal Organizers, Senior Move Managers, even Estate Liquidators, can be of help. These experienced individuals can be hired to help people sort through accumulated belongings, distribute and disperse what won't be needed in the new setting, and assist with all stages of packing, moving, and then unpacking and staging the new home. To be sensitive to the emotional implications of the move, they must allow time for discussion and decision-making. What will family members want to keep? Where and how to dispose of items no longer needed? Garage sale? Private sale or auction? Contributions to selected charities? Endless details. What, to do, for example, with those many framed family photographs that lined the long hallway all through the years? Maybe scan them and download them onto a digital picture frame that can be set on a table, continuously scrolling through the series.

Because moving seems to signify leaving behind a lifetime of memories, another talented professional may be called in, at a convenient time, to help capture and preserve the memories. Combining an individual's narrative with archival photos, these historians can help create personal history books to be treasured in the years ahead.

Without the trappings of the familiar, one must create a new life, bit by bit. But it is hard to do alone. Support from family members, friends, and even professionals is essential; and it does take time.

HOW TO BE TRANSPORTED?

Transportation is an important issue for seniors in America. A key ingredient for optimal adjustment in any living environment is the ability to get around. Cities today are woefully deficient in providing adequate transportation for the 20 percent of Americans over 65 who don't drive, and there is little federal funding available to help fill this need. Since women typically outlive their driving days by ten years this is of great concern to women in their 70's.

For walkers, streets and paths should be well lighted, and surfaces should be free of cracks, holes, and other impediments. Public buildings and recreational sites should have ramps and escalators. Badly needed for those still driving is larger print and better illumination of street and directional signs.

In small towns and suburban communities that were built for automobiles, and in cities everywhere, ideas are bubbling up for ways to transport older citizens who no longer drive. In areas of New York City, for example, school busses are appropriated during the day to carry adults to grocery shopping. The Dallas Area Agency on Aging has created the Community Transport Network with vehicles that provide lifts and ramps needed by those who have trouble with steps or are in wheelchairs.

The Independent Transportation Network (www.itnamerica. org) is a non-profit now in 27 communities in 21 states. It began in Maine in 1995, using paid and volunteer drivers to transport seniors and those with visual impairments. Silver Ride, in San Francisco (www.silverride.com), is a for-profit company that provides rides and social engagement for seniors. For about $85 for an average round trip, Silver Ride includes beyond intended destinations, outings like a movie or lunch with friends, while its drivers develop relationships with repeat riders and keep an eye out for changes in their health or behavior. In Denton County Texas, Special Programs for Aging Needs provides rides for adults over 60, for $5 per trip (www.SPAN-transit. org). Destinations include grocery stores, doctors' offices, hairdressers, libraries, etc. A case manager meets with potential riders to assess needs and set up a ride schedule. The county provides lift equipped vans, with volunteers aboard to help.

More electric scooter-type vehicles are available than ever before. There are several types and models:

Mobility Scooters are battery powered, motorized seats, useful for those who have difficulty walking, but they also can provide transportation for shorter errands for anyone willing to learn to use them.

Low Speed Vehicles (LSV's) are the models used at resorts, on golf courses, in master-planned communities, and on corporate campuses. Such zero-emission electric vehicles have a top speed of 25 MPH and are street legal in all 50 states for roads posted at 35 MPH.

Medium Speed Vehicles (MSV's) are 4-wheeled self-propelled electric vehicles that can be operated at up to 35 MPH on streets with a 40 MPH speed limit, or less, in the nine states that allow them. They meet federal safety standards including headlights, seat belts, a windshield, and a roll cage or crush proof body design.

Futuristic concepts in transportation and other next-generation technology will be explored and tested in a planned, smart city without people, in southwestern New Mexico.

WHAT TO DO WITH THIS GIFT OF TIME?

As they anticipate unscheduled free time after stopping work, senior women wonder what lies ahead. They have been used to having places to go, people to see and things to do, used to being busy, occupied with "important stuff," egos often fed by colleagues, students, and mentees. What now?

Women in 70Candles conversation groups said, *"Plenty."* They found there were still *"Never enough hours in the day."* Time released, it seems, fills like sands on the beach when the tide flows in. Choosing well is the challenge, they suggested.

Here is a generalized picture. Once a woman in her seventies has retired completely, or partially, from many years in a career or job that contributed to her identity in important ways, she has the opportunity to develop a new sense of herself and forge new roles. In the absence of structured plans, she might be surprised to experience a kind of foreground-background swap to her days. Time, that valuable commodity, previously carved and assigned in calendared bits, becomes wondrously unleashed.

Activities that were incidental unexpectedly become prominent events. There's time to savor morning coffee and the newspaper, moments to carefully fold laundry and actually reach the bottom of the laundry basket, opportunities to shop in the early hours of uncrowded supermarkets, and less need to multi-task. For some, this kind of interlude is refreshing and restorative. They relish the chance to read the books on their shelf, to have lunch with friends, and to spend time with a partner or grandchildren. Some, on the other hand, feel restless with the urge to use this ocean of time to channel their talents and energies into something they deem important.

Mostly, women in their 70's anticipate living longer than their grandmothers did and hope to make the best use of that gift of time by living well. The richness of existence then comes, not just from social connections, but also from larger causes where women contribute time, energy, and when possible, financial support. Among weekly activities are volunteer projects, such as tutoring in schools, mentoring, or engaging in political activism. They participate in charities in myriad roles and willingly spend time with grandchildren, demonstrating the generativity of this stage of life, as they share wisdom and life experience with that generation. Many engage in creative pursuits, reinvigorating old or discovering new modes of expression, in music, art, or dance. They improve balance, core stability and muscle strength at the gym, and treasure precious time for peaceful contemplation.

NEW LEARNING—Opportunities abound for women in their seventies to pursue new learning in local classes, in programs at local Adult Universities, through open on-line courses, in recreation centers, in religious sanctuaries, and in informal groups. A monthly book club becomes both a social and a literary wellspring, as members bond through years of get-togethers.

SENIOR CENTERS—Many towns have well-run Senior Centers open to anyone over fifty. For many, the very mention of the words "Senior Center" elicits an unpleasant vision, of old, dottering citizens, lonely and sad, with nowhere else to go. In fact, these are lively gathering places, more like day camp than nursing home. Seniors find companionship in a vast array of engaging activities. Something for every taste and temperament.

TRAVEL—Women are now traveling to new places with a renewed sense of wonder. Research reported by Bilger reveals that people focus longer on novelty and process those impressions more deeply in their brains. The brain's plasticity continues to create new, complex neural connections, with novel experiences. That's why new learning and travel are so enticing. Travel alters one's sense of time and offers a break from everyday, sometimes mindless, routines. Pillemer's Cornell Legacy Project interviews reveal that not travelling is one of the seniors' greatest regrets.

Travel provides a treasured sense of freedom and adventure, along with intellectual and cultural exploration. Women often read and study about their destination before they leave, enrich their knowledge of geography and history, and return with souvenirs, tales to tell, and indelible memories. One trip frequently leads to the next. Fellow travelers are often retirees, as well, and more than one lasting romance has bloomed among those widowed or divorced.

How refreshing it is to leave behind cars, cell phones and computers, to focus on a new here and now. New sounds, sights, aromas and rhythms—a parallel universe.

WHAT ABOUT HEALTH?

There are inevitable changes in women's bodies as they age. Women wonder, "What if I outlive my joints? Who knows what life-length these bodies were built for? Will there be ever more sophisticated replacement parts to set me back on my way?" Medical science has much to offer, with more on the horizon.

JOINTS—There are replacement knees, hips, and shoulders available. Remarkable limbs have been created now, even with mind-controlled movement.

ORGANS—Organs can be replaced as they falter. Liver, heart, lung, and kidney can be implanted. Surgical methods become more refined as doctors invent increasingly precise surgical techniques and engage robotic tools.

HEARING—What about sensorium? As hearing fades, sensitive digital hearing aids can compensate for sounds lost—If hearing fades completely, cochlear implants, partial or multi-channeled, are an option, to capture and deliver lost sounds again. And now, we read about promising research by Zhou and his team, on stem cells implanted in the cochlea of mice that regenerate lost hair cells and restore sound reception. Perhaps that will eventually work for humans.

VISION—As vision fades, eye glasses and contact lenses can provide correction—But what about more serious eye diseases?

Cataract surgery with lens implantation has become commonplace for people this age, and might even eliminate the need for eyeglasses. Treatment for incipient macular degeneration, however, still relies on vitamin pills to allay progression. Will stem cell implantation in the retina be next?

Fortunately, reading material can be enhanced in size, style, and brightness on Kindles and iPads, and various magnifying devices can be very beneficial. When all else fails, print-to-voice "readers" and audiobooks are available.

BALANCE—When balance becomes an issue, there are lots of devices to aid mobility: hikers' walking poles, various styles of canes, colorful walkers with wheels, seats, and utility baskets, and stairway chairlifts, in addition to the scooters described earlier.

MEDICAL EMERGENCIES—The needs of the older population require new solutions. Advances in the design of Emergency Rooms address those over 65, who account for a full 15-20% of emergency room visits, according to the MetLife Report. Efforts are being made to provide quiet settings with non-skid floors, hand rails, artificial skylight and darkness, and iPad devices for prompt communication with nurses.

HOW TO FACE THE END OF LIFE?

Women in their 70's hope to live well right up to the end of their lives. "Squaring off the curve" is the term Dr. Kenneth Cooper uses to describe how healthy, very old people contradict the traditional image of old age as a long slow decline.

But death is a shadow that can't be avoided. Each year, as family members and close friends die, women struggle, feeling the permanence of the loss. They try to come to terms with their experiences of death near them. Psychologists Ken and Mary Gergen speak about finding significance in such losses. They ask if we can "…find within our sorrows a deeper appreciation for the lives no longer with us…

Count the many ways in which they have enriched our lives and those of others." And they encourage us to appreciate our own suffering as a "tribute to those we have lost, and a signal of the depth of our relationship."

There are clergy, like Rabbi Dayle Friedman (www.growing-older.co) who specialize in the many social and spiritual issues related to old age. Rabbi Friedman among her other pastoral activities, leads a monthly group for women in their seventies, called Provisions for the Journey, where frank conversation focuses on spiritual and emotional preparation for the end of life. She offers inspiration and guidance in her book, *Jewish Wisdom for Growing Older (2015).*

There are several useful books available from women this age regarding these often emotion-laden topics. Letty Cottin Pogrebin (2013) offers advice about how to face, listen to, and talk with people who are sick and dying. Jane Brody (2009) writes about how to prepare for one's own demise. Further reading in their books finds suggestions about how to converse with doctors, how to make decisions about stopping treatment, about entering hospice, and how to thoughtfully prepare for the inevitable end of life.

We can also learn a great deal about health, the process of dying, and support from friends at death, from a wonderful group of nurses who have stayed in close touch through their 50 years post-graduation from their nursing college. Emily Mikulewicz, in a personal correspondence, wrote about her alumni group. Friends forever, these 25 women have met annually for social reunions and to chronicle life stages and health data in their ranks. They share and celebrate each other's joys and observe evolving health changes and illnesses with clinical acumen. Above all, they face these realities head on and provide heartfelt support in ways and times when it is needed—when friends are sick, and especially when death is imminent. She described how they treat the subject of death in their group.

> *"I can't imagine not talking about it, although I know a lot of people do not, and do not even acknowledge that a loved*

*one is dying, and so lose out on such important talk at the
end. We feel lucky as a group of friends, that we will have
each other's support when our time comes, without any
nonsense."*

Death Cafes, begun in England, have now spread to more than
22 countries, with more than a thousand cafes hosted to date (www.
deathcafe.com). The website describes their goal, "To increase awareness of death with a view to helping people make the most of their
finite lives." People gather weekly in informal, comfortable cafes or
restaurants, to have conversations about the often taboo subjects of
death and dying.

Although we know that death is part of life, facing the subject of
one's own demise is not easy. However, women do want to expand this
conversation, and new opportunities are emerging. Maybe the way has
finally been opened for this topic to be treated with "no nonsense."

TECHNOLOGY OF THE FUTURE

The digital world advances, regardless of any resistance. This
generation of women in their 70's is precariously sandwiched between
most of the World War II "greatest" seniors who refuse to have anything to do with the complications of the internet, and the boomers
behind who embrace everything electronic and ether-based. They've
witnessed an incredible swath of this evolution, as technological
change has run apace. Successive generations of devices both amaze
and unnerve, with alterations in ways to gather news, read books,
record ideas, contact friends, and listen to music.

Technology doesn't faze these woman completely. Most used
computers for years at work, and they now have grandchildren and
younger neighbors who can assist with the latest programs and high tech
gadgetry. But new items proliferate weekly, with sometimes mysterious
uses or applications, while flea markets and antique fairs display long
beloved desk phones, typewriters, vinyl records and radio consoles.

Since about one fourth of women 65 today will live to be 90 or so (Social Security Administration), it pays to peek ahead at technology of the future, for it may indeed describe a new world. In his book, *Physics of the Future: How Science will Shape Human Destiny and Our Daily Lives by the Year 2100,* Michio Kaku describes advances already in experimental stages. He sees incredibly rapid advancements that lie ahead through the wondrous sciences of computing, nanotechnology, artificial intelligence, biotechnology, and quantum theory. What a vision he has! There will no longer be individual computers or television sets. Instead, he describes wall screens everywhere. Home screens will provide access to people in any location and transmit whatever information a person might seek. Microchips will continue to increase capacity while they miniaturize further and reduce in cost. They can eventually become as small as a single atom, Kaku says, but along the way, tiny chips will be inserted on people, and in everything around them, including clothing, furniture, walls, appliances, signs, packaging, and on and on.

One's health will be constantly monitored, so there will be no need for that annual physical. Computers will absorb all the data continuously gathered from a person's body—and from monitors in their bathroom. The physician will be a robo-doc who appears on the wall screen of each home. Computers that constantly compare personal data with the best medical research and practice in the world will signal early warnings. The robo-doc will then refer a person to a specialist, in the earliest stages of any disorder.

NINA: THE PATH AHEAD

Given all that's on the horizon, what might a day in the life of a 70 year-old woman be like in the decades ahead? Let's imagine Nina...

Nina, whose husband died three years ago, lives in her own one-story home, in a pleasant intergenerational community, and intends to age in place. Her house is close to the village center where she's on a first name basis with the merchants in all the shops. Her extra bedroom welcomes visiting family members, but is available for a care-giver if ever that need arises.

As she awakens in the early morning, small LED lights automatically illuminate her pathway as she makes her way through the house. Her pre-set coffee begins to brew as she settles in her comfortable chair to peruse the morning news. The Google glasses she dons bring her a 3D experience of world events, as she changes channels with a nod of her head. A large screen on one wall brings a visit from her good friend, a life-size hologram, wishing her "Good morning" as they plan their day. Her friend views a hologram of Nina on her wall screen, at the same time.

As she inspects her fridge while preparing breakfast, Nina creates her shopping list by simply swiping an empty container across her refrigerator screen. When she presses "send" her list is electronically transmitted to the local grocery depot, where her order is processed and soon drone-delivered to her door. She prefers traditional fresh food, although she knows a popular line of meats is being produced from stem cells of animals. Her home food printer will create her main course for dinner. When it imports signals from the small skin implant on her arm, it will balance her nutritional need with her personal flavor and texture preferences. If she doesn't want to cook for herself, she knows she can eat out with friends, or have her favorite dishes sent to her from neighborhood restaurants. She sometimes helps deliver Meals-on-Wheels to older, house-bound elders; glad to know that service is available, should she ever need it.

For local errands, Nina likes to walk to the stores, wheeling her grocery tote as she goes. For more serious shopping, she accesses a motorized scooter at the nearby scooter sharing depot. Comfortably seated, she tells it where she needs to go, and she sits back as it automatically follows the magnetic strip in the roadway to her destination.

For more distant ventures, she signals the local ride service with a touch of her finger on her iBracelet. A car, having detected her location through its GPS, then promptly picks her up at her door, and later brings her home when she's ready. Today she's having lunch with old friends at a favorite bistro.

Although she is never one to rush to acquire the newest digital wonder, technology has gradually woven itself into the fabric of Nina's life. She doesn't miss a step when billboards and store window displays target her as she walks by, as they're triggered by her GPS. The device on her wrist responds to her voice requests as she uses it to phone, to locate destinations, to answer queries, to view pictures, and to hear music. When she is near a wall screen, she can project any of these functions to large visual displays...even conference calls. Until she had her cataracts repaired, she was glad to be able to project the book she was reading, upon her wall screen, or any other flat surface. Often, she added the audio component, allowing her to listen as she read along.

While she's away, her wrist device allows her to turn lights on and off in her home, alter the temperature setting, and check the premises, through cameras perched on her house and attached to her security drone. No more need for bulky keys or a wallet for money, as her digital ID lets her open any of her locks and buy and pay for items with the flick of her wrist.

Nina's not quite ready to get the newest contact lenses, but loves the idea that they can display, to her eyes only, the name and profile information of whomever she is facing. "Great for a cocktail party," she thinks. "The perfect antidote to a failing memory."

Not all of Nina's friends are as comfortable with this new technology. Some are still clinging to life as it used to be. Her pal Phyllis prefers books printed on paper and writes notes to people on pretty stationery. No wall screen at her house, but she knows how to e-mail her great-grandchildren on a still working, hand-me-down, first generation iPad. Nina notices, however that when they're together, Phyllis frequently asks her questions that can only be answered on a wrist device; Nina is happy to help her out.

Her health is monitored daily, at home, by tiny digital sensors in her cup, in her clothing, in her bathroom, and within her iBracelet, so doctor visits are infrequent when she is well. If the sensors register alarm, about blood pressure, cholesterol, body temperature, heartbeat, changes in saliva, or urine, her doctor is alerted electronically, and she receives a call for an appointment.

She's not one to complain about minor medical issues, but she's thankful for all the newest advances that are keeping her body functioning. Cataract surgery erased the sometimes beautiful, but also distracting, halos around all light sources and eliminated her need for eyeglasses. Her hip replacement was successful. No more grinding bone-on-bone that kept her up at night. And most amazing to her, just when she thought she would lose all her hearing in her right ear, she became a subject in a clinical trial that inserted stem cells, grown from her own skin, directly into her cochlea. Gradually, new cochlear hair cells were generated, and her hearing greatly improved. "What," she wondered, "will they think of next?"

Since she knows her family have concerns about her living alone, Nina has agreed to having a room sensor installed that alerts them to any drastic change in her daily movement. Her wrist device also functions as a life alert bracelet that would allow her to summon aid in an emergency. Her family also knows that she is regularly taking her prescribed medications, as she, and they, receive feedback messages from her digitized pill dispenser.

When she recently had a fall and needed assistance during her recovery, a mobile robot was available to help Nina move about, get dressed, and clean up the house when her home health aide was not there. She still is happy to have the robo-vac on active duty while she's out.

Nina loves to garden, and she delights in having the neighborhood children join her at harvest time. She shares her vegetable bounty with her friends and neighbors, and her home is cheered by the colorful fresh flowers she grows.

Her day begins with a nearby exercise class, often followed by coffee with some of her classmates. They like to talk about books they are reading, places they've been, family matters, and current events. They disperse to carry on their busy lives.

On her way home, Nina stops to visit her 97 year old aunt, who is being well-cared for in a Green Home Project house where she lives with eleven other "elders," each with their own private room and bath. They share an airy central living room. With no fixed schedule to obey, her aunt enjoys sleeping late and likes to help out in the large, open communal kitchen. The residents and nursing aid staff can eat and socialize together at a single, long dining table. Her aunt's mobility has recently improved greatly after a tiny electrical stimulator was implanted on her vagus nerve, to reduce the inflammation caused by her arthritis.

Each week, Nina enjoys volunteering at a local 1st grade class where she reads with the students and teaches them songs she knows. She sings in a local choir and enjoys being part of their performances in the town's church.

In the summer, five generations of her large family gather at a beach house for a week of swimming and hanging out. Occasionally, one or two of her great-grandchildren will come and stay with her for a few days.

Nina plays cards with a group at her local senior center, goes to concerts with her good friend, and tries her hand at painting classes in her town. She loves good books, good films, good food, and travel adventures. Although she is no longer on her town council, she remains politically active in her community and involved in local issues.

Nina treasures her quiet time at home. She often avails herself of an afternoon nap, but is then up and out to her evening activities. She's enjoying these years without a constricting office schedule, and she has no intention of slowing down. She knows these years are precious. She has friends who are taking the new wonder drugs that slow the aging process, and they marvel at the unique breed of tiny jellyfish that never dies, but lives forever. But Nina has made all needed plans for the end of her life and continues to make the best of the time she has.

FINALE

We've tried, in this book, to reach a better understanding of the lives of women in their 70's. We've described a Senior Adult Stage of life, in light of our increased longevity, and we've imagined what our world will look and feel like in the decades ahead. Our picture is a mostly positive one, of women active, healthy, and optimistic. Although we know there are many who are struggling with ill-health, financial calamities, loss, loneliness, or depression, we've seen the power in women's friendships that can mitigate much of that suffering. Perhaps we've offered ideas that will be of help to Boomers who will want to live as well as possible in their eighth decade, and of course beyond.

Our blog and our groups represent but a small piece of American society. Now it's time to evaluate women in their 70's in other socio-economic groups, other cultures, and other nations. We hope this effort will stimulate further study.

APPENDICES

Appendix A- Invitation

What It's Like to be 70-ish and Female in 2012

Please join us for a gathering of women our age for a conversation about this era in our lives.

Ellen Cole, of Albany and Jane Giddan, of Dallas will be in New York City to convene the next in a series of interactive groups about the joys and challenges of being 70.

This is an extension of our web blog at 70Candles.com.

We hope to put together a book that will offer the boomer generation of women a road map of what's ahead for them.

We invite you to join us

[DATE]

[TIME]

[LOCATION]

We promise an interesting time, with warm-hearted observations and sharing.

Refreshments will be served.

Space will be limited.

RSVP to janegiddan@gmail.com

Appendix B—Information Cards

Information Cards for 70Candles Gatherings

AGE:

HIGHEST DEGREE: High School____ Bachelors___ Masters____
Professional___

WORK STATUS: FT____ PT_____ Retired_____

LENGTH OF CAREER_____

MARITAL STATUS: Single____ Married_____ Divorced_____
Widowed_____

CURRENT LIVING: Urban_____ Suburban_____ Rural_____
House____ Apt_____ Condo_____ Community Living_____

WHAT DO YOU WANT TO BE SURE WE TALK ABOUT
TODAY?

Appendix C-Ages of Women

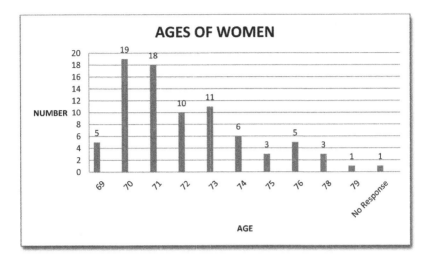

Appendix D- Educational Levels

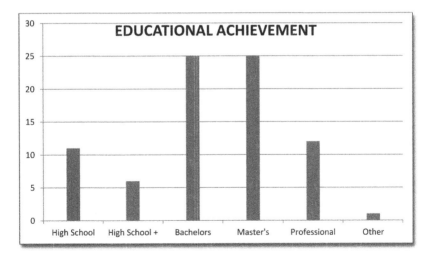

Appendix E- Length of Careers

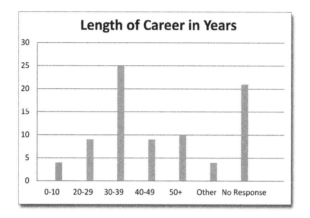

Appendix F- Demographics

82 PARTICIPANTS

Location				Age		
Dallas 1	12	15%		69	5	6%
New York 1	12	15%		70	19	23%
New York 2	9	11%		71	18	22%
Ithaca	11	13%		72	10	12%
Philadelphia	13	16%		73	11	13%
Albany 1	9	11%		74	6	7%
Albany 2	8	10%		75 +	12	15%
Dallas 2	8	10%		No Response	1	1%

Length of Career				Marital Status		
0-10	4	5%		Married	47	57%
20-29	9	11%		Divorced	20	24%
30-39	25	30%		Widowed	11	13%
40-49	9	11%		Single	4	5%
50+	10	12%				
Other	4	5%				

Highest Degree				Work Status		
High School	11	13%		Full Time	9	11%
Bachelors	25	30%		Part time	17	21%
Masters	25	30%		Retired	47	57%
Professional	12	15%		Actively Retired	9	11%
No Response	2	2%				
High School+	6	7%				
Other	1					

Housing Locale				Housing Type		
Urban	22	27%		House	49	60%
Suburban	37	45%		Apartment	12	15%
Rural	6	7%		Condo	13	16%
No Response	17	21%		Town House	3	4%
				No Response	5	6%

Appendix G- Living Long

BLUE ZONE	INTERHEART STUDY- All controllable risks	SCOTT	FORDHAM CENTENARIAN STUDY
Move naturally	Smoking	1. Do you have an elderly relative-95+?	1. Meaningfulness
Know your purpose	High blood-pressure	2. How fast and far can you walk?	2. The will to live-with No problem talking about death and dying
Shed stress	Lipids	3. Do you have a lot of people in your life?	3. High levels of self-efficacy-a sense of being able to fulfill their needs and accomplish their goals
Eat a Mediterranean diet	Diabetes	4. Are you a woman?	5. Optimism-looking forward to their lives
Stop eating when 80% full	Abdominal obesity	5. Did you have a child after 35?	
Drink in moderation	Sedentary life style	6. When were you born?	
Practice your faith	Alcohol (+ or -)	7. Do you worry, but not too much?	
Put families first	Few fruits and vegetables	8. Weight normal- or slightly overweight?	
Stay social		9. How long are your telemeres?	

Appendix H- Living Well

RATH & HERTER	PILLEMER	VAILLANT	BUTLER	SELIGMAN
Career Well-being	1. Career with intrinsic rewards	1. Social utility	1. Maintain mental vitality	Positive emotions
Social Well-being	2. Good health habits	2. Tolerance for old age	2. Nurture relationships	Engagement
Financial Well-being	3. Say "yes" to opportunities	3. Hope	3. Seek essential sleep	Relationships
Physical Well-being	4. Choose a mate with extreme care	4. Joy and Humor	4. Minimize stress	Meaning
Community Well-being	5. Travel more	5. Past & Present	5. Connect with your community	Accomplishments
	6. Say it now	6. Intimacy	6. Live an active life	
	7. Live as though life is short		7. Eat healthfully	
	8. Happiness is a choice		8. Practice prevention	
	9. Don't worry			
	10. Savor simple pleasures			

Appendix I- Challenge of Change

CHALLENGE OF CHANGE
1. Identity: Personal, Social, Family, Vocational (job/career, home-maker)
2. Changes in Function: Health, Physical Aging
3. Viewed by Others

Appendix J- Growth Over Time

GROWTH OVER TIME
1. Life now—TODAY
2. Advice to Younger Women—YESTERDAY
3. Thriving in our Later Eighth and Ninth Decades—TOMORROW

REFERENCES

Introduction

Pillemer, K. (2011). *30 lessons for living: Tried and true advice from the wisest Americans.* New York: Hudson Street Press.

Chapter One

Lapham, L.H. (October 26, 2014). Old Masters. Justice Ruth Bader Ginsburg. *The New York Times Health Issue.* p. 41.

Reivich, K. & Shatte, A. (2002).*The resilience factor: 7 keys to finding your inner strength and overcoming life's hurdles.* New York: Broadway Books.

Chapter Three

AARP. Biography of AARP's founder, Ethel Percy Andrus. Retrieved from http://assets.aarp.org/www.aarp.org_/articles/NRTA/andrus_bio.pdf

Barzilai, N. & Rennert, G. (October 31, 2012). The rationale for delaying aging and the prevention of age-related diseases. *Rambam Maimonidies Med. J.* 10087. Retrieved from http://www.ncbi.nlm.nih.gov/pmc/articles/PMC3678824

Buettner, D. (2012). *The Blue Zones, Second edition: 9 lessons for living longer from the people who've lived the longest.* Washington DC: National Geographic.

Butler, R. N. (1975). *Why survive? Being old in America.* New York: Harper and Row.

Carstenson, L. L. (2009). *A long bright future: An action plan for a lifetime of happiness, health, and financial security.* New York: Broadway Books.

Erikson, E. (1959). *Identity and the life cycle: Selected papers.* Psychological Issues Monograph Series, Vol. I, Whole No. 1. New York: International Universities Press.

Hall, S. S. (May 2013). Longevity. *National Geographic Magazine.* Retrieved from http://ngm.nationalgeographic.com/2013/05/longevity/hall-text

Joop, D. S. (2010-2012). Psychological strengths in centenarians: Mechanisms of adaptation in the very old. Fordham Centenarian Study (Research in process), Retrieved from http://legacy.fordham.edu/academics/programs_at_fordham_/psychology_departmen/people/faculty/

daniela_jopp/adult_development_an/research_projects/project_psychologica_77836.asp

Kabat, G. (May 29, 2013). Why do some people live to 100 years? *Forbes*. Retrieved from www.forbes.com/sites/geoffreykabat/2013/05/29/why-do-some-people-live-to-100-years/

Kjaersgaard, K. (2005). Aging to perfection or perfectly aged? The image of women growing older on television. In E. Cole & J. Henderson Daniel (Eds.), *Featuring females: Feminist analyses of media* (pp. 199-210). Washington, D. C.: American Psychological Association.

Levinson, D. J. (1996). *Seasons of a woman's life.* New York: Alfred A. Knopf.

Levy, B. R., Slade, M. D., Kunkel, S. R., & Kasl, S. V. (2002). Longevity increased by positive self-perceptions of aging. *Journal of Personality and Social Psychology, 83*(2), 261-270. doi: 10.1037/0022-3514.83.2.261.

McLeod, S. A. (2008). *Eric Erikson/ Psychosocial Stages—Simply Psychology,* Retrieved from http://www.simplypsychology.org/Erik-Erikson.html

Meyer, J. (December 2012). 2010 Census Special Reports, *Centenarians: 2010,* C2010SR-03, Washington, DC: U.S. Government Printing Office. Retrieved from www.census.gov/prod/cen2010/reports/c2010sr-03.pdf

Pillemer, K. (2011). *30 lessons for living: Tried and true advice from the wisest Americans.* New York: Hudson Street Press.

Rath, T., & Herter, J. (2010). *Well Being: The five essential elements.* New York: Gallup Press.

Scott, P. S. (2011). 10 surprising clues you'll live to be 100, Retrieved from www.Caring.com

Seligman, M. E. P. (2011). *Flourish: A visionary new understanding of happiness and well-being.* New York. Free Press.

Terrill, L. & Gullifer, J. (2010). Growing older: A qualitative inquiry into the textured narratives of older, rural women. *Journal of Health Psychology,* 15, 707-715.

Vaillant, G. E. (2002). *Aging well.* New York: Little Brown and Co.

Www.census.gov/population/www/documentation/twps0049/tabA-1.pdf

Yusuf, S., Hawken, S., Ounpuu, S., Dans, T., Avezum, A., Lanas, F. INTERHEART Study Investigators. (2004). Effect of potentially modifiable risk factors associated with myocardial infarction in 52 countries (the INTERHEART study): Case controlled study. *The Lancet. 364*: 9438, 937-952.

Chapter Four

Allen, A. B. & Leary, M. R. (2013). Self-compassionate responses to aging. *The Gerontologist*, doi:10.1093/geront/gns204

Ball, K., Berch, D. B., Helmers, K. F., Jobe, J. B., Leveck, M. D., Marsiske, M., & Willis, S. L. (2002). Effects of cognitive training interventions with older adults: A randomized controlled trial. *JAMA*, 288(18), 2271-2281.

Barzilai, N. & Rennert, G. (October 31, 2012). The rationale for delaying aging and the prevention of age-related diseases. *Rambam Maimonidies Med. J.* 10087. Retrieved from http://www.ncbi.nlm.nih.gov/pmc/articles/PMC3678824

Baum, S. K. (1997). Review of The seasons of a woman's life by Daniel J. Levinson. *Journal of Adult Development, 4*(1), 55-56.

Bonanno, G. A., Wortman, C. B., Lehman, D. R., Tweed, R. G., Haring, M., Sonnega, J., Nesse, R. M. (2002). Resilience to loss and chronic grief: A prospective study from preloss to 18-months postloss. *Journal of Personality and Social Psychology, 83*(5), 1150-1164.

Bookwala, J. & Jacobs, J. (2004). Age, marital processes, and depressed affect. *The Gerontologist, 44*(3), 328-338.

Bowling, A. & Dieppe, P. (2005). What is successful ageing and who should define it? *British Journal of Medicine, 3311*, 1548-1551.

Brody, J. (2009). *Jane Brody's guide to the great beyond: A practical primer to help you and your loved ones prepare medically, legally and emotionally for the end of life.* New York: Random House.

Buettner, D. (Sept/Oct 2009) Live more good years. AARP The Magazine, Retrieved from www.aarp.org/health/longevity/info-09-2009/more_good_years.html

Buettner, D. (2012). *The Blue Zones, Second edition: 9 lessons for living longer from the people who've lived the longest.* Washington DC: National Geographic.

Buhler, C. (1935). The curve of life: Life as studied in biographies. *Journal of Applied Psychology, 19*, 405-409.

Bush, K.M., Machinist, L.S., & McQuillan, J. (2013). *My house our house: Living far better for less on a cooperative household.* Pittsburgh, PA: St. Lynn's Press.

Callanan, M. & Kelley, P. (2012). *Final gifts: Understanding the special awareness, needs and communications of the dying.* New York: Simon & Schuster Paperbacks.

Carstenson, L. L. (2009). *A long bright future: An action plan for a lifetime of happiness, health, and financial security*. New York: Broadway Books.

Carstensen, L. L., Gottman, J. M., & Levenson, R. W. (1995). Emotional behavior in long-term marriage. *Psychology and Aging, 10*(1), 140-149. doi: 10.1037/0882-7974.10.1.140.

Cole, E. & Gergen, M. (Eds.). (2012). *Retiring but not shy: Feminist psychologists create their post-careers*. Chagrin Falls, OH: Taos Institute Publications.

Davis, J. C., Marra, C. A., Beattie, B. L., Robertson, M. C., Najafzadeh, M., Graf, P., Liu-Ambrose, T. (2010). Sustained cognitive and economic benefits of resistance training among community-dwelling senior women: A 1-year follow-up study of the Brain Power Study. *Archives of Internal Medicine, 170*(22), 2036-2038. doi:10.1001/archinternmed.2010.462.

de Beauvoir, S. (1972). *The coming of age*. New York: G. P. Putman's & Sons.

Durrett, C. (2009). *The senior cohousing handbook, 2nd Edition: A community approach to independent living*. Gabriola Island, BC, Canada: New Society Publishers.

Epstein, C. F. (1971). Review of "The woman doctorate in America" by Helen S. Astin. *American Journal of Sociology, 77*(2), 359-361.

Erikson, E. H. & Erikson, J. M. (1997). *The life cycle completed (Extended version)*. New York: W.W. Norton & Company.

Erikson, E. H., Erikson, J. M., & Kivnick, H. Q. (1986). *Vital involvement in old age*. New York: Norton.

Friedan, B. (1993). *The fountain of age*. New York: Simon & Schuster.

Friedman, E. M., Hayney, M. S., Love, G. D., Urry, H. L., Rosenkranz, M. A., Davidson, R. J. & Ryff, C. D. (2005). Social relationships, sleep quality, and interlukin-6 in aging women. *Proceedings of the National Academy of Science, 102*(51), 18757-18762.

Frieze, I. H., Olson, J. E., & Murrell, A. J. (2011). Working beyond 65: Predictors of late retirement for women and men MBAs. *Journal of Women & Aging, 23*, 40-57. doi:10.1080/08952841.2011.540485.

Glass, A. P (2009). Why aging in community? In C. Durrett (Eds.), *The senior cohousing handbook: A community approach to independent living* (Appendix A). Gabriola Island, BC, Canada: New Society Publishers.

Goodman, E. (January 1, 2010). Ellen Goodman writes of letting go in her final column. Retrieved from http://www.washingtonpost.com/wp-dyn/content/article/2009/12/31/AR2009123101743_2.html

Hays, T., Bright, R., & Minichiello, V. (2002). The contribution of music to positive aging. *Journal of Aging and Identity, 7*(3), 165-175.

Hays, T. & Minicchiello, V. (2005). The meaning of music in the lives of older people: A qualitative study. *Psychology of Music, 33*, 437-451. doi: 10.1177/0305735605056160

Helson, R., Jones, C., & Kwan, V. S. Y. (2002). Personality change over 40 years of adulthood: Hierarchical linear modeling analyses of two longitudinal samples. *Journal of Personality and Social Psychology, 83*(3), 752-766.

Huppert, F. (2009). *The science of high performance ageing.* The Meyler Campbell Annual Lecture 2009. Retrieved from http://www.meylercamp-bell.com/programmes/lecture2009.html

Huppert, F. A., Abbott, R. A., Ploubidis, G. B., Richards, M., & Kuh, D. (2009). Parental practices predict psychological well-being in mid-life: Life-course associations among women in the 1946 British birth cohort. *Psychological Medicine*, 1-12. doi:10.1017/S0033291709991978.

Johnson, J. K. & Mutchler, J. E. (2013). The emergence of a positive geron-tology: From disengagement to social involvement. *The Gerontologist,* doi: 10.1093./geront/gnt099

Joop, D. S. (2010-2012). Psychological strengths in centenarians: Mechanisms of adaptation in the very old. Fordham Centenarian Study (Research in process), Retrieved from http://legacy.fordham.edu/aca-demics/programs_at_fordham_/psychology_departmen/people/faculty/daniela_jopp/adult_development_an/research_projects/project_psycho-logica_77836.asp

Kaku, M. (2012). *Physics of the future: How science will shape human destiny and our daily lives by the year 2100.* New York: Doubleday.

Katz, S. & Marshall, B. (2003). New sex for old: Lifestyle, consumerism, and the ethics of aging well. *Journal of Aging Studies, 17*, 3-16.

Kelland, K. (July 3, 2013). Scientists create human liver from stem cells. London: Reuters. Retrieved from www.reuters.com/article/2013/07/03/us-liver-stemcells-idUSBRE9620Y120130703

Kern, M. L. & Friedman, H.S. (2010). Why do some people thrive and others succumb to disease and stagnation? Personality, social relations, and resilience. In P. S. Fry & C. L. M. Keyes (Eds.), *Frontiers of resilient aging* (pp. 162-184). New York: Cambridge University Press.

Krause, N. (2006). Gratitude toward God, stress, and health in late life. *Research on Aging, 28*(2), 163-183.

Lang, I. Wallace, R. B., Huppert, F. A., & Melzer, D. (2007). Moderate alcohol consumption in older adults is associated with better cognition and well-being than abstinence. *Age and Ageing, 36*(3), 256-261. doi:10.1093/ageing/afm001

Levinson, D. J. (1996). *Seasons of a woman's life.* New York: Alfred A. Knopf.

Levy, B. R., Slade, M. D., Kunkel, S. R., & Kasl, S. V. (2002). Longevity increased by positive self-perceptions of aging. *Journal of Personality and Social Psychology, 83*(2), 261-270. doi: 10.1037/0022-3514.83.2.261.

Lightfoot-Lawrence, S. (2009). *The third chapter: Passion, risk, and adventure in the 25 years after 50.* New York: Farrar, Straus and Giroux.

Lindau, S. T., Schumm, L. P., Laumann, E. O., Levinson, W., O'Muircheartaigh, C. A., & Waite, L. J. (2007). A study of sexuality and health among older adults in the United States. *New England Journal of Medicine, 357,* 762-774.

MetLife Report on Aging in Place 2.0: Rethinking Solutions to the Home Care Challenge (2010). In conjunction with Louis Tenenbaum, CAPS, CAASH, Independent Living Strategist, Retrieved from https://www.metlife.com/assets/cao/mmi/publications/studies/2010/mmi-aging-place-workbook.pdf

Meyer, J. (December 2012). 2010 Census Special Reports, *Centenarians: 2010,* C2010SR-03, Washington, DC: U.S. Government Printing Office. Retrieved from www.census.gov/prod/cen2010/reports/c2010sr-03.pdf

Mussen, P., Eichorn, D. H., Honzik, M. P., Bieber, S. L., & Meredith, W. M. (1980). Continuity and change in women's characteristics over four decades. *International Journal of Behavioral Development, 3,* 333-347.

Neff, K. D. & Germer, C. K. (2013). A pilot study and randomized controlled trial of the Mindful Self-compassion Program. *Journal of Clinical Psychology, 69,* 28-44.

Peterson, C. (2005). *A primer in positive psychology.* New York: Oxford University Press.

Peterson, C., Park, N., & Seligman, M. E. P. (2006). Greater strengths of character and recovery from illness. *The Journal of Positive Psychology, 1*(1), 17-26.

Pillemer, K. (2011). *30 lessons for living: Tried and true advice from the wisest Americans.* New York: Hudson Street Press.

Pion, G. M., Mednick, M. T., Astin, H. S., Iijima Hll, C. C., Kenkel, M. B., Keita, G. P., & Kelleher, J. C. (1996). The shifting gender composition of psychology. *American Psychologist, 51*(5), 509-528.

Pogrebin, L. C. (1996). *Getting over getting older.* Boston: Little Brown

Pogrebin, L. C. (2013). *How to be a friend to a friend who's sick.* New York: Public Affairs.

Price, C. A. (2000). Women and retirement: Relinquishing professional identity. *Journal of Aging Studies, 14*(1), 81-101.

Rich, J. P. (Ed.). (2012). *Cornell class of 1962-50th reunion yearbook.* New York: JPR Communications.

Rosenfeld, J. & Chapman, W. (2008). *Home design in an aging world.* New York: Fairchild Books, Inc.

Rountree, C. (1999). *On women turning 70: Honoring the voices of wisdom.* San Francisco, CA: Jossey-Bass.

Salamon, J. (2011). *Wendy and the lost boys: The uncommon life of Wendy Wasserstein.* New York: Penguin Press.

Seligman, M. E. P. (2011). *Flourish: A visionary new understanding of happiness and well-being.* New York. Free Press.

Slevin, K. F. & Wingrove, C. R. (1995). Women in retirement: A review and critique of empirical research since 1976. *Sociological Inquiry, 65*, 1-21.

Smith, G. (2013). A boy and his bot. *Rise of the robots.* New York: Time Inc. Specials. pp. 92-102.

Smith, G. J. W. & van der Meer, G. (1990). Creativity in old age. *Creativity Research Journal, 3*(4), 249-264. doi: 10.1080/10400419009534359.

Stone, A. A., Schwartz, J. E., Broderick, J. E., & Deaton, A. (2010). A snapshot of the age distribution of psychological well-being in the United States. *Proceedings of the National Academy of Sciences (PNAS).* Published online before print May 17, 2010, doi: 10.1073/pnas.1003744107.

Terrill, L. & Gullifer, J. (2010). Growing older: A qualitative inquiry into the textured narratives of older, U. S. Census Bureau, Population Division (2010). Retrieved from http://www.census.gov/population/www/socdemo/age/

Vaillant, G. (2004). Positive aging. In P. A. Linley & S. Joseph (Eds.), *Positive psychology in practice* (pp. 561-578). New York: Wiley.

Vaillant, G. E. (2002). *Aging well.* New York: Little Brown and Co.

Wink, P. & Helson, R. (1997). Practical and transcendent wisdom: Their nature and some longitudinal findings. *Journal of Adult Development, 4*(1), 1-15.

Wykle, M. L. & Gueldner, S. H. (Eds.). (2011). *Aging well: Gerontological education for nurses and other health professionals.* Sudbury, MA: Jones & Bartlett Learning.

Vortman, K. (January 21, 2013). The operating room of the future. *Insightec.* Retrieved from https://search.yahoo.com/yhs/sea rch?p=vortman+the+operating+room+of+the+future&ei= UTF-8&hspart=mozilla&hsimp=yhs-003

Chapter Five

Abrahms, S. (April 30, 2013). Improving transportation services for seniors. *AARP Bulletin.* Retrieved from http://www.aarp.org/home-family/getting-around/info-04-2013/seniors-independent-living-public-transportation.html

Abrahms, S. (June, 2013). Sharing home sweet home. *AARP Bulletin.* pp. 16-19.

Administration on Aging (2013). Older Americans Act. Department of Health and Human Services. Retrieved from http://www.aoa.gov/AoA_Programs/OAA/Introduction.aspx

Agronin, M. (2011). *How we age: A doctor's journey into the heart of growing old.* Cambridge, MA: DaCapo Press.

Behar, M. (May 25, 2014). Invasion of the body hackers. *The New York Times Magazine.* pp. 36-41.

Bilger, B. (April 25, 2011). The Possibilian. New York: *The New Yorker*, p. 12.

Blow, S. (April 21, 2012). Dr. Kenneth Cooper says physical fitness helps even in death. Dallas: *The Dallas Morning News,* Retrieved from http://www.dallasnews.com/news/columnists/steve-blow/20120421-dr.-kenneth-cooper-says-physical-fitness-helps-even-in-death.ece

Brody, J. (2009). *Jane Brody's guide to the great beyond: A practical primer to help you and your loved ones prepare medically, legally and emotionally for the end of life.* New York: Random House.

Buettner, D., (2012). *The Blue Zones, Second edition: 9 lessons for living longer from the people who've lived the longest.* Washington DC: National Geographic.

Bush, K.M., Machinist, L.S., & McQuillan, J. (2013). *My house our house: Living far better for less on a cooperative household.* Pittsburgh, PA: St. Lynn's Press.

Clausing, J. (May 12, 2012). If they build it, no one will come. *The Dallas Morning News*, p.3A.

Cooper, K. & Cooper, T. (2007). *Start strong, finish strong: Prescription for a lifetime of great health*. New York: Penguin Group.

Davis, L. S. (June-July, 2013) Age-proofing the burbs. *AARP The Magazine*.

Dunn, J. (August-September 2014). Declutter your life-Now! *AARP The Magazine*, pp. 39-42.

Friedan, B. (1993). *The fountain of age*. New York: Simon & Schuster.

Friedman, D.A. (2015). *Jewish wisdom for growing older: Finding your grit and grace beyond midlife*. Woodstock, VT: Jewish Lights Publishing.

Gergen, K. & Gergen, M. (March/April 2013). *Positive Aging Newsletter*. The Taos Institute. Issue No. 79.

Jacobs, M. (November 22, 2011). When there's no place like home. *The Dallas Morning News, Senior Living*. p. 10.

Jaffe, I. (July 24, 2013). Move over nursing home—there's something different. *NPR*. Retrieved from http://www.npr.org/2013/07/24/196249703/move-over-nursing-homes-theres-something-different

Kaku, M. (2012). *Physics of the future: How science will shape human destiny and our daily lives by the year 2100*. New York: Doubleday.

Landry, R. (2014). *Live long, die short: A guide to authentic health and successful aging*. Austin, TX: Greenleaf Book Group Press.

McCamant, K. & Durrett, C. (1988). *Cohousing: A contemporary approach to housing ourselves*. Berkeley, CA: Ten Speed Press.

MetLife Report on Aging in Place 2.0: Rethinking Solutions to the Home Care Challenge (2010). In conjunction with Louis Tenenbaum, CAPS, CAASH, Independent Living Strategist. Retrieved from https://www.metlife.com/assets/cao/mmi/publications/studies/2010/mmi-aging-place-workbook.pdf

MetLife Report. (April 15, 2012). *The Dallas Morning News*. p. 4A.

National Council on Aging (2013). Administration on Aging, Department of Health and Human Services. Retrieved from http://www.aoa.gov/

Neergaard, L. (July 11, 2011), Aging America living in cities built for the young. *The Dallas Morning News* p. 7A, The Associated Press.

Park, A. (2013) Walking wonders: Robotic appendages are helping paralyzed patients and amputees regain everyday functions. pp. 86-91. In *Rise of the robots*. New York: Time Inc. Specials.

Pillemer, K. (2011). *30 lessons for living: Tried and true advice from the wisest Americans*. New York: Hudson Street Press.

Pogrebin, L. C. (2013). *How to be a friend to a friend who's sick*. New York: Public Affairs.

Rich, N. (December 2, 2012). Forever and ever. *The New York Times Magazine*. pp. 32-39

Rosenfeld, J. & Chapman, W. (2008). *Home design in an aging world*. New York: Fairchild Books, Inc.

Schacter-Shalomi, Z. S. & Miller, R. (1995). *From Aging to Sage-ing: A revolutionary approach to growing older*. New York: Warner Books.

Social Security Administration. Calculators: Life Expectancy. Retrieved from http://www.ssa.gov/planners/lifeexpectancy.html

Thomas. W.H. (2004). *What are old people for?* Acton, MA: VanWyk Burnham.

U.S. Department of Housing and Urban Development. Evidence Matters. Retrieved from www.huduser.org/portal/periodicals/em/fall13/highlight1.html

Yip, P. (July 22, 2013). Reliable transportation key for healthy seniors. *The Dallas Morning News*. pp. 1D & 4D

www.atlantaregional.com/aging-resources

www.av.clubexpress.com/

www.changingaging.org

www.cohousing.org/directory/view/21478

www.deathcafe.com

www.edenalt.org

www.eldercohousing.org

www.friendscentercity.org

www.growingolder.co

www.itnamerica.org

www.meetup.com/Aging-In-Community/events/74588922/

www.roommates4boomers.com

www.silverride.com

www.SPAN-transit.org

www.thegreenhouseproject.org

www.thetransitionnetwork.org

Yadegaran, J. (January 15, 2014). Death café: Talk about dying and eat cake too. *San Jose Mercury News*. Retrieved from www.mercurynews.com/bay-area-living/ci_24918825/death-café-talk-about-dying-and-eat-cake-too

Zhou, Y., Yuan, J., Zhou, B., Lee, A. J., Lee, A. J., Ghawji, M. Jr., & Yoo, T. J. (2011). The therapeutic efficacy of human adipose tissue-derived mesenchymal stem cells on experimental autoimmune hearing loss in mice. *Immunology, 133*(1), 133-140.

ACKNOWLEDGMENTS

We have so many people to thank for bringing this book to life. Foremost are the women who so graciously hosted our 70Candles conversation groups and those who brought their friends to the gatherings: G. Nannette Ashe, Paulette Baxter, Gail Cammer, Evelyn Eskin, Alice Hernandez, Hyacinth Mason, Helen Mora, and Shelli Taub. We appreciate Temple Beth Emeth of Albany, New York, and the Cathedral de Guadalupe in Dallas, Texas, for their assistance in our efforts. Our scribes Vedan Anthony-North, Karen Lovelace, Renee Newton, and Pascale Stain were our angels. We are greatly indebted to our readers, Ginnie Bivona, Becky Bouchard, Evelyn Eskin, Lynn Paulson, Sara Powers, and Alison Schmerler, who generously gave of their time and provided editing and honest appraisals of our writing at various stages of this book's development. We do not have words sufficient to thank Mary Gergen who told us, "Yes, you need to publish this book."

For kind permission to use their prose and poetry, we thank Emily Mikulewicz, Caroline M. Simon, Maggy Simony, Maureen Sze, and Marion Sobel on behalf of Dora V. Gordon.

When we set out this journey, Renee Jain enthusiastically helped us establish our 70Candles on-line blog. Every 70 year-old needs a younger partner or two when it comes to the electronic world, and we lucked out with ours.

The thoughts and words of the many participants in our 70Candles conversation groups, and contributors to our 70Candles blog, are the heart of this project. We have used fictitious names to assure their anonymity, but we know they will recognize themselves as they read. Our hats off as well to all the old women we have known, loved, and admired, and for the inspiration they have provided.

We both gain tremendous strength and encouragement from our wonderful husbands, Norman Giddan and Doug North, who remain ever loving and supportive through the (many) decades.

~ Jane Giddan and Ellen Cole

ADDITIONAL READINGS

Bateson, M. C. (2010). *Composing a further life: The age of active wisdom*. New York: Vintage Books.

Butler, R. N. (2010). *The longevity prescription: The 8 proven keys to a long, healthy life*. New York: Avery.

Chast, R. (2014). *Can't we talk about something more pleasant?* New York: Bloomsbury.

Cohen, H. J. (2000). *Taking care after 50: A self-care guide for seniors*. New York: Three Rivers Press.

Cowley, M. (1981). *The view from 80*. Boston: G.K.Hall Co.

Cozolino, L. (2008). *The healthy aging brain: Sustaining attachment, attaining wisdom*. New York: W.W. Norton & Company.

Davis, N.D., Cole, E., & Rothblum, E.D. (Eds.). (1993). *Faces of women and aging*. New York: Harrington Press, Inc.

DuFouil, C. (July 14, 2013). INSERM- French Government Health Research Agency. Presentation at the Alzheimer's Association International Conference, Boston.

Ephron, N. (2010). *I remember nothing and other reflections*. New York: Knopf.

Fleisher, M. & Reese, T. (2013). T*he new senior woman: Reinventing the years beyond mid-life*. Lanham, MD: Rowman & Littlefield.

Fonda, J. (2011). *Prime time*. New York: Random House.

Franks, J. (2014). *To move or to stay: A guide for your last decades*. Seattle, WA: University book Store Press.

Gawande, A. (2014). *Being mortal: Medicine and what matters in the end*. London: Profile Books Ltd.

Groen, J. A. & Rizzo, M. J. (2003). *The changing composition of American-citizen PhDs*. Paper prepared for conference "Science and the University," Cornell Higher Education Institute, Ithaca, NY, May 20-21, 2003.

Gruenwald, T. L., Liao, D.H., & Seeman, T.E. (2012). Contributing to others, contributing to oneself: Perceptions of generativity and health in later life. *The Journal of Gerontology, Series B. Psychological Sciences and Social Sciences. 67*, (6): 660-665.

Klimaski, J. (July 16, 2012). Centenarian study investigates the well-being paradox. *Inside Fordham*. New York: Fordham University, Retrieved from http://legacy.fordham.edu/campus_resources/enewsroom/inside_fordham/july_16_2012/news/centenarian_study_in_88272.asp

Moon, S. (2010). *This is getting old: Zen thoughts on aging with humor and dignity*. Boston: Shambhala.

O'Connor, S. (Ed.). (2015). *Secrets of living longer*. New York: Time Inc. Books.

Park, A. (2013). Walking wonders: Robotic appendages are helping paralyzed patients and amputees regain everyday functions. pp. 86-91. In *Rise of the robots*. New York: Time Inc. Specials.

Pawelski, J. O. (September 9, 2010). Foundations of Positive Interventions, MAPP 602. Class Lecture, University of Pennsylvania.

Post, M. (April, 2012). Cultured meat from stem cells: Challenges and prospects. *Meat Sciences 92*(3): 29 7-301.

Rappoport. A. (January 25-31, 2012). Milestone e-news.

Reichman, J. (1996). *I'm too young to get old*. New York: Random House.

Repko, M. (November 22, 2011). Design for the ages, *The Dallas Morning News,* Senior Living. p.14.

Sellers, R. (2013). *Seventy things to do when you turn 70*. South Portland, Maine: Sellers Publishing.

Satran, P. R. (2009). *How not to act old: 185 ways to pass for phat, sick, hot, dope, awesome, or at least not totally lame.* New York: Harper Collins.

Taylor, S. E., Klein, L. C., Lewis, B. P., Gruenewald, T. L., Gurung, R. A., & Updegraff, J. A. (2000). Biobehavioral responses to stress in females: Tend-and-befriend, not fight or flight. *Psychological Review, 107*(3), 4111-429.

The Transition Network and Gail Rentsch. (2008). *Smart women don't retire-they break free*. New York: Springboard Press.

Thone, R. R. (1992). *Women and aging: Celebrating ourselves*. New York: Harrington Park Press.

Thomas, B. (2014). *Second wind: Navigating the passage to a slower, deeper and more connected life*. New York: Simon & Schuster.

University of British Columbia (December 14, 2010). Strength training for seniors provides cognitive function, economic benefits. *Science Daily*. Retrieved from www.sciencedaily.com/releases/2010/12/101213163810.htm

Vaillant, G. E. & Vaillant, C. O. (1990). Determinants and consequences of creativity in a cohort of gifted women. *Psychology of Women Quarterly, 14*, 607-616.

Viorst, J. (2005). *I'm too young to be seventy and other delusions.* New York: Free Press.

RELEVANT WEB SITES

http://70candles.com

http://agesong.com

http://Authentichappiness.com

http://beingseventy@blogspot.com

http://bridgetable.net

http://Caring.com

http://cohousing.org

http://Comingofage.org

http://cooperativeaging.com

http://Elderchicks.com

http://elderspirit.net

http://elderwisdomcircle.org

http://Fiercewithage.com

http://Globalaging.org

http://Graypanthersnyc.org

http://huffingtonpost.com/jane-giddan-and-ellen-cole/

http://legacyproject.human.cornell.edu

http://lifereimagined.aarp.org

http://Longevity.stanford.edu

http://owch.org.uk

http://Poeticsofaging.org

http://roadscholar.org

http://secondjourney.org

http://Seniornetworkalliance.com

http://Silversneakers.com

http://Theconversationproject.org

http://Thethirdact.net

http://vital-aging-network.org

ABOUT THE AUTHORS

Jane Giddan, M.A.,CCC-SLP, a speech-language pathologist and educator, trained at Cornell and Stanford, is a fellow of the American Speech Language and Hearing Association and professor emerita of the Department of Psychiatry, Medical College of Ohio. She has specialized in language development and disorders, is an international consultant on autism, and has co-authored numerous articles and books including, *European Farm Communities for Autism*, and *Childhood Communication Disorders in Mental Health Settings*. Still a clinician, but also mother of two and engaged grandmother of three, she has recently created some environmentally focused children's books with her husband, Norman. From her home in Dallas Texas, she continues to write, and blogs at 70Candles.com and Huff/Post50 as she composes her semi-retirement life.

Ellen Cole, PhD, is a psychologist who has specialized in women's mental health and human sexuality. She is professor of psychology emerita at Alaska Pacific University in Anchorage and currently holds the position of Professor of Psychology at the Sage Colleges in Albany and Troy, NY. At age 70 she earned a second master's degree in Applied Positive Psychology from the University of Pennsylvania, and so began her interest in "positive aging." Ellen is former editor of the journal *Women and Therapy*, a fellow of the American Psychological Association, and past president of the Alaska Psychological Association and APA's Division 35, the Society for the Psychology of Women. She is currently Book Review Editor for the journal *Psychology of Women Quarterly*. Her most recent book, co-edited with Mary Gergen, is *Retiring But Not Shy: Feminist Psychologists Create Their Post-Careers*. Married to Doug North, and living in Albany, New York, she is mother of four and grandmother of ten.

TAOS INSTITUTE PUBLICATIONS

Taos Tempo Series:
Collaborative Practices for Changing Times

70Candles! Women Thriving in Their 8th Decade, (2015) by Jane Giddan and Ellen Cole (also available as an e-book)

U&ME: Communicating in Moments that Matter, New & Revised! (2014) by John Stewart (also available as an e-book)

Relational Leading: Practices for Dialogically Based Collaboration, (2013) by Lone Hersted and Kenneth J. Gergen (also available as an e-book)

Retiring But Not Shy: Feminist Psychologists Create their Post-Careers, (2012) edited by Ellen Cole and Mary Gergen (also available as an e-book)

Developing Relational Leadership: Resources for Developing Reflexive Organizational Practices, (2012) by Carsten Hornstrup, Jesper Loehr-Petersen, Joergen Gjengedal Madsen, Thomas Johansen, Allan Vinther Jensen (also available as an e-book)

Practicing Relational Ethics in Organizations, (2012) by Gitte Haslebo and Maja Loua Haslebo

Healing Conversations Now: Enhance Relationships with Elders and Dying Loved Ones, (2011) by Joan Chadbourne and Tony Silbert

Riding the Current: How to Deal with the Daily Deluge of Data, (2010) by Madelyn Blair

Ordinary Life Therapy: Experiences from a Collaborative Systemic Practice, (2009) by Carina Håkansson

Mapping Dialogue: Essential Tools for Social Change, (2008) by Marianne "Mille" Bojer, Heiko Roehl, Mariane Knuth-Hollesen, and Colleen Magner

Positive Family Dynamics: Appreciative Inquiry Questions to Bring Out the Best in Families, (2008) by Dawn Cooperrider Dole, Jen Hetzel Silbert, Ada Jo Mann, and Diana Whitney

Focus Book Series

*A Student's Guide to Clinical Supervision: You are not Alone, (*2014) by Glenn E. Boyd (also available as an e-book)

When Stories Clash: Addressing Conflict with Narrative Mediation, (2013) by Gerald Monk, and John Winslade (also available as an e-book)

Bereavement Support Groups: Breathing Life into Stories of the Dead, (2012) by Lorraine Hedtke (also available as an e-book)

The Appreciative Organization, Revised Edition (2008) by Harlene Anderson, David Cooperrider, Kenneth J. Gergen, Mary Gergen, Sheila McNamee, Jane Watkins, and Diana Whitney

Appreciative Inquiry: A Positive Approach to Building Cooperative Capacity, (2005) by Frank Barrett and Ronald Fry (also available as an e-book)

Dynamic Relationships: Unleashing the Power of Appreciative Inquiry in Daily Living, (2005) by Jacqueline Stavros and Cheri B. Torres

Appreciative Sharing of Knowledge: Leveraging Knowledge Management for Strategic Change, (2004) by Tojo Thatchenkery

Social Construction: Entering the Dialogue, (2004) by Kenneth J. Gergen, and Mary Gergen (also available as an e-book)

Appreciative Leaders: In the Eye of the Beholder, (2001) edited by Marge Schiller, Bea Mah Holland, and Deanna Riley

Experience AI: A Practitioner's Guide to Integrating Appreciative Inquiry and Experiential Learning, (2001) by Miriam Ricketts and Jim Willis

Books for Professionals Series

Social Constructionist Perspectives on Group Work, (2015) edited by Emerson F. Rasera

New Horizons in Buddhist Psychology: Relational Buddhism for Collaborative Practitioners, (2010) edited by Maurits G.T. Kwee

Positive Approaches to Peacebuilding: A Resource for Innovators, (2010) edited by Cynthia Sampson, Mohammed Abu-Nimer, Claudia Liebler, and Diana Whitney

Social Construction on the Edge: 'Withness'-Thinking & Embodiment, (2010) by John Shotter

Joined Imagination: Writing and Language in Therapy, (2009) by Peggy Penn

Celebrating the Other: A Dialogic Account of Human Nature, (reprint 2008) by Edward Sampson

Conversational Realities Revisited: Life, Language, Body and World, (2008) by John Shotter

Horizons in Buddhist Psychology: Practice, Research and Theory, (2006) edited by Maurits Kwee, Kenneth J. Gergen, and Fusako Koshikawa

Therapeutic Realities: Collaboration, Oppression and Relational Flow, (2005) by Kenneth J. Gergen

SocioDynamic Counselling: A Practical Guide to Meaning Making, (2004) by R. Vance Peavy

Experiential Exercises in Social Construction – A Fieldbook for Creating Change, (2004) by Robert Cottor, Alan Asher, Judith Levin, and Cindy Weiser

Dialogues About a New Psychology, (2004) by Jan Smedslund

WorldShare Books – Free PDF Download

Post-modern Education & Development (Chinese edition, PDF version 2014) Introduction by Shi-Jiuan Wu (後現代教育與發展　　介紹 吳熙琄)

Exceeding Expectations: An Anthology of Appreciative Inquiry Stories in Education from Around the World (PDF version 2014) Story Curators: Dawn Dole, Matthew Moehle, and Lindsey Godwin

The Discursive Turn in Social Psychology (PDF version 2014), by Nikos Bozatzis & Thalia Dragonas (Eds.)

Happily Different: Sustainable Educational Change – A Relational Approach (PDF version 2014), by Loek Schoenmakers

Strategising through Organising: The Significance of Relational Sensemaking, (PDF version 2013), by Mette Vinther Larsen

Therapists in Continuous Education: A Collaborative Approach, (PDF version 2013), by Ottar Ness

Contextualizing Care: Relational Engagement with/in Human Service Practices, (PDF version 2013), by Janet Newbury

Novos Paradigmas Em Mediação (PDF versión 2013, original publicación date 1999), Dora Fried Schnitman y Stephen LittleJohn (editors)

Filo y Sofía En Diálogo: La poesía social de la conversación terapéutica (PDF version 2013, original publicación date 2000), Klaus G. Deissler y Sheila McNamee (editors). Traducción al español: Mario O. Castillo Rangel

Socially Constructing God: Evangelical Discourse on Gender and the Divine (PDF version 2013), by Landon P. Schnabel

Ohana and the Creation of a Therapeutic Community (PDF version 2013), by Celia Studart Quintas

From Nonsense Syllables to Holding Hands: Sixty Years as a Psychologist (PDF version 2013), by Jan Smedslund

Management and Organization: Relational Alternatives to Individualism (PDF version 2013, reprinted with permission) Edited by Dian Marie Hosking, H. Peter Dachler, Kenneth J. Gergen

Appreciative Inquiry to Promote Local Innovations among Farmers Adapting to Climate Change (PDF version 2013) by Shayamal Saha

La terapia Multi–Being. Una prospettiva relazionale in psicoterapia, (PDF version 2013) by Diego Romaioli

Psychotherapy by Karma Transformation: Relational Buddhism and Rational Practice (PDF version 2013) by G.T. Maurits Kwee

La terapia como diálogo hermenéutico y construccionista: Márgenes de libertad y deco-construcción en los juegos relacionales, de lenguaje y de significado (PDF versión 2012) by Gilberto Limón Arce

Wittgenstein in Practice: His Philosophy of Beginnings, and Beginnings, and Beginnings (PDF version 2012) by John Shotter

Social Construction of the Person (PDF version 2012). Editors: Kenneth J. Gergen and Keith M. Davis, Original copyright date: 1985, Springer-Verlag, New York, Inc.

Images of Man (PDF version 2012, original copyright date: 1975) by John Shotter. Methuen, London.

Ethical Ways of Being (PDF version 2012). By Dirk Kotze, Johan Myburg, Johann Roux, and Associates. Original copyright date: 2002, Ethics Alive, Institute for Telling Development, Pretoria, South Africa.

Piemp (PDF version 2012), by Theresa Hulme. Published in Afrikaans.

Etnia Terapéutica: Integrando Entornos (PDF version 2015) by Jeannette Samper A. and José Antonio Garciandía I.

Buddha As Therapist: Meditations (PDF version 2015), by G.T. Maurits Kwee

For book information and ordering, visit Taos Institute
Publications at:
www.taosinstitutepublications.net

For further information, call: 1-888-999-TAOS, 1-440-338-6733
Email: info@taosinstitute.net

Lightning Source UK Ltd.
Milton Keynes UK
UKOW06f1700270416

273099UK00005B/358/P